The Newport Cookbook

Newport, Rhode Island, has had a remarkable and exciting history that spans several eras of American history, and each era was characterized by its cuisine. In colonial Newport the early settlers blended traditional English dishes with Indian customs. They refined the delicate jonny cake and made wonderful breads with cornmeal. They cooked game and fresh garden vegetables and made pickles and relishes and fine cheeses. Authentic recipes for these and other early delights of the table appear in THE NEWPORT COOKBOOK.

When the city became a seaport, trading vessels brought spices, fruits from southern climates, and exotic delicacies, and the cuisine of Newport took on a new dimension. The first resorters, lured by the lovely climate, came to dine lavishly at the newly built hotels on beefsteak pie, pork with horseradish applesauce, lobster salad, and charlotte russe. The clambake ritual was created.

Picnics and parties in the late 1800's meant competition among hosts and hostesses to serve the most elaborate and delectable meals. French chefs prepared *huîtres gratinées à la crème* (creamed oysters), *noisettes d'agneau cussy* (boned and rolled lamb chops with artichoke hearts with mushroom puree), and *gâteau meringue* (meringue cake). If Newport seemed elegant in the 1870's and 1880's, however, it would appear provincial in retrospect at the turn of the century. Spectacularly ornate summer cottages were built in what had now become the queen of resorts. Dinner parties featured the finest of French *haute cuisine*. A party on board William K. Vanderbilt's yacht, *Alva*, featured *Oeufs à l'Aurore, Langouste à la Newburg, Tournedos à la Moelle, Petit Poulet Grillé au Cresson*, and *Crêpes aux Confitures*.

THE NEWPORT COOKBOOK is an evocative display of Americana. Each era is described and illustrated with etchings and photographs that recall periods of the country's history. Authentic recipes from each era– clearly and skillfully presented to be made today – provide a treasury of superb dishes.

Ceil Dyer worked closely with The Preservation Society of Newport County in researching and writing THE NEWPORT COOKBOOK. She has written widely on food subjects and is the author of *The Quick Gourmet Cookbook,* among a number of other fine cookbooks.

THE NEWPORT COOKBOOK

by Ceil Dyer

Foremost Publishers
Little Compton, Rhode Island

Copyright © MCMLXXII by Ceil Dyer
Library of Congress Catalog Card Number: 72-39252
All rights reserved.
Published by Foremost Publishers,
Little Compton, R.I. 02837
Formerly published by Weathervane Books
a division of Barre Publishing Company, Inc.
by arrangement with Hawthorn Books, Inc.
a b c d e f g h
Manufactured in the United States of America
ISBN 0-940078-08-2
Cover photo — Courtesy of Richard Cheek, photographer
and Magazine, Antiques

Contents

PART I

Of Sailing Ships and Sealing Wax

PART II

Of Cottages and Kings

v

PART I

Of Sailing Ships and Sealing Wax

Roger Williams (1599–1683), the founder of Rhode Island (*The Picture Decorator, Inc.*)

CHAPTER 1

In the Beginning

One of the first things we know about the New World adventures of Roger Williams, the founder of the Rhode Island colony, was that he was welcomed by the Indians and invited to a meal of boiled fish and succotash. Ever since, boiled fish of some kind—often mackerel or herring—along with that classic mixture of corn and beans, has been a favorite Rhode Island menu. Before the first white settlers came to what is now Newport, the Indians who lived there depended almost entirely upon the bounties of nature. Though they did practice a form of agriculture which amounted to little more than planting kernels of corn in holes and hilling them up with stone implements, they principally ate what could be killed in the forest, what could be dug from the soft mud and sandy shores nearby, what could be speared in the shallow waters, and what grew in season on trees, bushes, and vines.

It wasn't long, however, before Newport's settlers developed what were called plantations. These were actually

Roger Williams is welcomed by the Indians. (*The Rhode Island Historical Society*)

produce-raising farms that imported beef, cattle, and swine from England. Nonetheless, bear meat and venison were still found on the tables of these pioneers, and cod and mackerel, captured in the homespun seine, were kept in the salt barrel.

As for flour and meal for bread, biscuits, and flapjacks, there was the town miller a mile or two up the road. Heavy sacks of corn and wheat had to be hauled to the miller's great revolving stones; the flour and cornmeal had to be carted back again and carefully stored to keep away moisture and mice. Newport's housewives added to the variety of their daily fare by pickling and preserving the fruit and corn of summer and the autumn harvest of apples, cranberries, and squash. According to early accounts, the preserves, pickles, and relishes were so rich and spicy that there was little need to make the jars and containers airtight.

The plantation cows produced a great surplus of milk, particularly during the summer months, and since the perishable nature of the product made shipment impossible under the prevailing conditions, this surplus milk was converted into cheese. By the middle of the eighteenth century great quantities of cheese were produced and exported, not only to the other American colonies but to Europe as well. Robert Hazard, of South County fame, had as many as twelve Negro women who, each with an assistant, did nothing but make cheese. These women produced twelve to twenty-four large wheels of cheese a day in his extensive dairy.

By 1750 cheese-making was well established, and it continued to be a principal product of Narragansett County until after the Napoleonic Wars, when, as the county expanded, it became more profitable to convert excess milk into butter to be sold locally. Fine homemade cheese, however, continued to be a housewives' art until the late 1800's. An interesting comment on Narragansett's cheese is in-

A KEY into the
LANGUAGE
OF
AMERICA:
OR,

An help to the *Language* of the *Natives*
in that part of AMERICA, called
NEW-ENGLAND.

Together, with briefe *Observations* of the Cu-
stomes, Manners and Worships, &c. of the
aforesaid *Natives*, in Peace and Warre,
in Life and Death.

On all which are added Spirituall *Observations*,
Generall and Particular by the *Authour*, of
chiefe and speciall use (upon all occasions) to
all the *English* Inhabiting those parts;
yet pleasant and profitable to
the view of all men :

BY ROGER WILLIAMS
of *Providence* in *New-England.*

LONDON,
Printed by *Gregory Dexter*, 1643.

Roger Williams's *A Key into the Language of America*, with perhaps the first recipes from the new world (*The John Carter Brown
Library, Brown University, Providence, Rhode Island*)

6

Excerpts from *A Key into the Language of America*:

"Whomever cometh in when they [Indians] are eating, offer them to eat of that which they have, though but little enough prepared for themselves. If any provision of fish or flesh, come in, they make their neighbours partake with them. If any stranger comes in, they presently give him to eat of what they have; many a time, and at all times of the night (as I have fallen in travel upon their houses), when nothing hath been ready, have themselves and their wives risen to prepare me some refreshing."—Chapter II

"*Nokehick*, parched meal, is ready and very wholesome food, which they eat with a little water, hot or cold. I have travelled with neere 200 of them at once, neere 100 miles through the woods, every man carrying a little basket of this at his back, and sometimes in a hollow leather girdle about his middle, sufficient, for a man three or four daies. With this readie provision, and their bows and arrows, are they ready for war and travel at an hour's warning. With a spoonful of this meal and a spoonful of water from the brook have I made many a good dinner and supper."—Chapter II

"*Nasaump* is a kind of meale pottage, unparched. From this the English call their Samp, which is the Indian corne beaten and boiled and eaten hot or cold with milk or butter, which are mercies beyond the native's plaine water and which is a dish exceeding wholesome for the English bodies."—Chapter II

"From thick warm valleys where they winter, they remove a little nearer to their fields, where they plant corn . . . the worke of one field is over, they remove house to the other. If death falls in amongst them, they presently remove to a fresh place. If an enemy approach, they remove into a thicket or swamp unless they have some fort to remove into. . . . Their great remove is from their summer fields to warme and thicke wooded bottoms where they winter. They are quick, in half a day yes, sometimes at a few houres warning, to be gone and they house up elsewhere, especially if they have stakes readie pitched for their mats. . . . The men make up the poles or stakes, but the women make and set up, take down, order and carry the mats and household stuff."—Chapter VI

"The Indians have an abundance of these sorts of Fowle upon their waters, take great pains to kill any of them with their Bow and Arrowes."—Chapter XV

"The Indians have an art of drying chestnuts and so to preserve them in their barns for a daintie all the year. They also dry acorns . . . by much boyling they make a good fish of them. . . . The strawberry is the wonder of all the fruits growing naturally in these parts. . . . The Indians bruise them in a morter, mix them with meale and make Strawberry bread. . . . The women set or plant, weede and hill, gather and barne all the corn and fruits of the field . . . when a field is to be broken up. They have a very loving sociable, speedy way to dispatch it. All the neighbors, men and women, forty, fifty, a hundred, join and come in to helpe freely. With friendly joining they break up their fields, build their forts, stop and kill fish in the rivers. . . . The Indian women use their natural hoes of shells and wood. The women of a family will commonly raise two or three heaps of corn . . . twelve, fifteen and twenty bushels in each heap, which they drie in round, broad heaps . . . covering it with mats at night and opening it when the sun is hot."—Chapter XVI

cluded in a letter from Benjamin Franklin to one Miss
Katherine Ray. It reads:

> All our friends have tasted it, and all agree that it exceeds
> any English cheese. Mrs. Franklin was very proud that a
> young lady should have so much regard for her old husband
> [Franklin was then forty-nine] as to send him such a present.
> She is sure you are a very sensible girl, and a notable house-
> wife, and talks of bequeathing me to you as a legacy, but I
> ought to wish you a better, and hope she will live these
> hundred years; for we are grown old together, and if she
> has any faults, I am so used to them that I don't perceive
> them; as the song says:
>> Some faults have we all, and so has my Joan,
>> But then they're exceedingly small;
>> And now I'm grown used to them, so like my own,
>> I scarcely can see them at all. . . .

From the founding of Newport through the eighteenth
century, Newporters blended their English food heritage
with that of the Indians. English recipes for puddings and
pies, such as slump, were made with the native blueberries
rather than with the more familiar English fruits. Instead
of roast goose, there was turkey; instead of plum pudding,
Indian pudding made of cornmeal. Basically, however, the
daily fare of the settlers was inherited from seventeenth-
century England; it was changed only to accommodate to
the ingredients that were native to the New World—simply
because they were available, and the more familiar ones
were not to be had. The blending was a happy one, and
although the roots of the following collection of recipes
are English, they reflect the ingenuity of those early housewives who used what was at hand to create a uniquely
American cuisine.

ફ➤

RHODE ISLAND FISH CHOWDER
(very old recipe)

1 pound salt pork, cut into thin strips
4 pounds fillet of cod or sea bass, cut into 4-inch squares
4 medium onions, peeled and chopped
½ cup chopped parsley
1 tablespoon chopped fresh savory (or 1 teaspoon dried
  ground savory)
Cayenne pepper
2 cups crumbled soda crackers
Boiling water
Butter
½ cup pearl barley
2 tablespoons butter
1 tablespoon flour
Salt
Pepper

Cover the salt pork with cold water; bring to a boil, then let simmer for 5 minutes. Drain.

Cover the bottom of a chowder kettle with a layer of pork; place on this a layer of fish and then a layer of chopped onion. Sprinkle with some of the parsley and savory and with cayenne pepper to taste. Top with a layer of crumbled soda crackers and pour on enough boiling water to moisten the crackers. Dot the surface with butter as needed, then repeat the layering process, starting with salt pork and ending with crackers, water, and butter until all the ingredients have been used. Sprinkle the barley, which has been washed in a sieve under cold running water until the water runs clear, over the final layer of crackers. Add sufficient boiling water to cover all the ingredients. Cover the kettle and cook over low heat for 1 hour, watching to see that the level of water does not sink too low. Should the top layer become exposed and dry, add more boiling water.

When ready to serve, ladle the solids into a large soup tureen and keep warm.

Cream the 2 tablespoons butter with the flour to make a paste. Add to the remaining liquid in the kettle and stir until blended and smooth. Correct seasoning with salt and pepper as needed. Bring to a boil and pour immediately over the contents of the tureen.

Serve at once.

Makes 8 to 10 servings.

ॐ

CODFISH CAKES

Salt codfish was a staple of the Newport colonists, and codfish cakes made a frequent appearance at the table, especially for breakfasts, which were always substantial. Very likely the earliest codfish cakes did not have cream or eggs and were, no doubt, cooked in poultry fat instead of oil, but few will quarrel about the minor change in the classic recipe.

1 pound salt cod
2 pounds boiling potatoes
6 tablespoons butter
1 medium onion, peeled and very finely chopped
¼ cup finely minced parsley
3 egg yolks
2 tablespoons heavy cream
½ teaspoon freshly ground black pepper
Vegetable oil, for frying

Place the cod in a nonmetal bowl and cover with water. Let soak 6 to 8 hours, draining and covering with fresh water about every 2 hours.

Cut the cod into 2-inch squares. Place in a saucepan and cover with water. Bring to a boil, then lower heat and let simmer for about 20 minutes, or until the fish flakes easily when tested with a fork. Drain.

Remove the skin and bones and flake the fish with a fork into fine shreds.

Peel and dice the potatoes. Place in a saucepan with 1 inch of boiling water. Cover and cook until the potatoes are tender. Drain and place in a large mixing bowl. Mash until smooth.

Meanwhile, melt the butter in a second saucepan. Add the onion and parsley. Sauté until the onion is limp. With a rubber spatula scrape the entire contents of the pan into the bowl of hot mashed potatoes.

In a small bowl beat the egg yolks with the cream. Add to the potato mixture and beat until smooth. Add the flaked cod, season with the pepper, and blend well.

Pour sufficient oil into a large heavy saucepan to a depth of about 3 inches. Heat to 375° F. on a deep-frying thermometer.

Drop the codfish mixture, a tablespoon at a time, into the hot fat. Fry the balls 5 or 6 at a time for 3 to 4 minutes, or until they are golden on all sides. Drain on paper toweling and keep hot in a shallow pan lined with paper towels in a warm oven until all the remaining cakes are fried.

Makes 6 to 8 servings.

ॐ

A SWINGING CRANE AND BUBBLING POT
HIGH-NOON BOILED DINNER
(original recipe)

"First make sure the fire is good and steady, such as will last until dinner is served. As soon as breakfast is well out of the way, hang on a big pot half full of cold water, and put in a piece of corned beef and a chunk of salt pork. About nine, if the water is boiling hard, put in the pudding, being careful that the cloth has been dipped in scalding water, squeezed dry and floured, before the pudding is placed in it. Put in the beets about the same time. At half-past eleven parsnips and potatoes and squash cut in quarters on top. Serve the pudding first, with butter and molasses. Then dish up the dinner, with beef and pork in the middle of the platter, and the vegetables arranged around them in tasty manner."

ॐ

BOILED DINNER

Even today a boiled dinner is best when cooked in a pot hung on a crane over an open fire in the fireplace. Such cooking has a flavor all its own. Nonetheless, if properly prepared, a boiled dinner done on top of the stove is still mighty fine eating . . . especially on a cold snowy day in New England.

The White Horse Tavern, at the corner of Farewell and Marlborough streets, was probably built before 1673. William Mayes, Sr.
(whose son was a pirate), had been granted a license to keep a
tavern as early as 1687. By 1708 the town council was "sitting at the
house of Robert Nichols," and town records show that the cost of
the council dinners prepared by Nichols came out of the town
treasury from 1708 to 1712. During the ensuing years the old building became so much a center of the town's affairs that when the
new Colony House was being planned, the question arose as to
whether it should be built facing the tavern rather than the bay.
The legislators compromised: The capitol building faced the harbor, but its north side door faced the side door of the tavern a
block away. While the Colony House was under construction, the
General Assembly, as well as a criminal court, met at "Jonathan
Nichols Inn." (*The Preservation Society of Newport County, Newport, R.I.*)

1 4-pound brisket of beef
Boiling water
6 to 8 very small white onions, peeled
6 to 8 very small carrots, scraped
4 medium potatoes, peeled and cut into 2-inch pieces
4 small turnips, peeled and cut into 2-inch pieces
4 small squashes, peeled and cut into 2-inch pieces
1 small cabbage, trimmed, cored, and cut into wedges
Salt
Pepper
Hot mustard
Horseradish Sauce (see page 15)
Skillet Corn Bread (see pages 50–51)

Tie the brisket of beef securely into shape with butcher's string, or have your butcher do this for you.

Place the beef in a large pot and add sufficient boiling water to come to about 3 inches of the rim. Let simmer over a low heat for about 2 hours and then add the onions, carrots, and potatoes; continue to simmer. After another 15 minutes add the turnips and squashes. After simmering for about another 45 minutes, or when the meat and all the vegetables are tender, add the cabbage and cook a final 15 minutes.

Slice the meat and place it in the center of a large platter. Surround it with the vegetables and sprinkle all with the salt and pepper. Season the cooking broth to taste.

Serve the meat and vegetables in shallow soup plates, with some of the broth ladled over them. Have hot mustard and Horseradish Sauce on the table and pass a bread basket filled with wedges of crispy hot-from-the-oven Skillet Corn Bread.

Makes 8 servings.

NOTE: The meat will slice nicely if taken from the broth and allowed to stand for about 15 minutes before serving.

Horseradish Sauce

3 tablespoons butter
3 tablespoons flour
2 cups boiling stock from Boiled Dinner pot
2 tablespoons prepared horseradish

Melt the butter in a saucepan over a moderate heat. Stir in the flour and blend well. Slowly add the boiling stock, stirring as it is added.

Cool, stirring until thick and smooth. Remove from the heat and stir in the horseradish.

Makes 8 servings.

ȝ∾

ROAST TURKEY WITH CORN-BREAD AND OYSTER STUFFING

Roast turkey with savory stuffing was an early tradition in all of New England, and Newport was no exception. Plump, fresh-killed birds, stuffed and then roasted in the great brick ovens of the kitchen buildings adjoining the manor houses, appeared on colonial Newport tables from early fall to late spring. Corn-bread stuffing often replaced the wheat-bread stuffing of old England in the early days, as wheat flour for bread was still scarce, but this was more cause for rejoicing than otherwise, for the corn-bread flavor was soon regarded as even more delectable.

1 9-pound freshly killed turkey
1 teaspoon salt
Corn-Bread and Oyster Stuffing (see pages 17–18)
6 tablespoons melted chicken fat
4 tablespoons melted butter
Gravy for Roast Turkey (see page 18)

Preheat oven to 425° F.

Wash the turkey quickly under cold running water and clean the cavity of all extraneous tissues. Reserve the gizzards, heart, and liver for the stuffing. Dry the turkey thoroughly, inside and out, with paper toweling. Sprinkle the cavity with the salt.

Fill both the breast cavity and the neck cavity loosely with the stuffing. (Resist overstuffing, or it will surely escape and spoil the appearance of your bird; leftover stuffing may be baked separately in a well-buttered dish.) Close the openings with small metal skewers or sew them together with a large needle and strong white butcher's thread. Truss the bird securely.

Place the bird on its side on a rack in a large roasting pan. Cover with a piece of cheesecloth which has been soaked in the melted chicken fat and butter.

Roast for 15 minutes, then turn the bird on the other side and roast for another 15 minutes, again covering it with the fat-soaked cheesecloth.

Lower the temperature to 375° F. and continue to roast for about 2 hours. Turn the bird often. Resoak the cheesecloth in melted chicken fat and butter as necessary. Remove the cheesecloth for the last half hour of cooking time. Pierce the thigh to test for doneness. If the juice that runs out is clear, with no tinge of pink, the bird is done.

Remove the turkey to a carving platter and allow to stand 15 to 20 minutes before carving. Serve with a sauce boat of the Gravy.

Makes 8 to 10 servings.

Corn-Bread and Oyster Stuffing

Gizzards, heart, and liver of turkey
1 small onion, peeled and quartered
1 stalk celery with leaves, finely chopped
1 bay leaf
5 or 6 peppercorns
⅓ teaspoon salt
4 cups water
5 cups crumbled Skillet Corn Bread (see pages 50–51)
5 tablespoons butter
½ cup finely chopped onion
½ cup finely chopped celery
1 pint oysters, drained and chopped
1 egg, lightly beaten
Salt
Freshly ground black pepper

Place the gizzards, heart, and liver in a 3- to 4-quart saucepan. Add the quartered onion, celery stalk, bay leaf, peppercorns, ⅓ teaspoon salt, and water. Bring to a boil, then lower the heat, partially cover the pan, and simmer. Remove the heart and liver after 30 minutes of cooking; set aside. Continue to simmer until the gizzards are tender —about another 1½ hours. Strain the cooking broth and set aside; discard the solids. When the broth is cool, skim off the fat.

Coarsely chop the gizzards, heart, and liver; reserve the gizzards for the Gravy. Add the heart and liver to the crumbled Skillet Corn Bread in a large mixing bowl.

In a small skillet melt the butter. Add the ½ cup chopped onion and ½ cup chopped celery and sauté until the vegetables are limp. With a rubber spatula scrape the entire contents of the skillet into the Corn Bread mixture.

Stir in the oysters and add the egg, then add about

¼ cup at a time of the strained cooking broth, enough to make a moist dressing. Reserve about 2 cups broth for the Gravy. Season lightly with salt and pepper. Blend well before stuffing the turkey.

Makes 8 to 10 servings.

Gravy for Roast Turkey

2 tablespoons flour
*2 cups turkey broth (see recipe for Corn-Bread and Oyster
    Stuffing, page 17)*
*Chopped cooked gizzards (see recipe for Corn-Bread and
    Oyster Stuffing)*

After removing the turkey from the oven, skim off all but a thin film of fat from the roasting pan. Place the pan over a low heat on top of the stove and stir the flour into the fat. Cook, stirring for 2 to 3 minutes and scraping in the brown particles clinging to the bottom and sides of the pan. Then add the broth, stirring as it is added.

Add the gizzards and stir over a high heat until the sauce is thick and smooth.

Makes 8 to 10 servings.

RHODE ISLAND BAKED BEANS

*2 pounds (4 cups) dried pea beans (or Great Northern
    beans)*
3 to 4 quarts water
1 large onion, peeled and chopped

1 piece (8 ounces) lean, mildly cured salt pork
2 tablespoons cider vinegar
1 cup dark-brown sugar
½ cup dark molasses
2 teaspoons salt
1 teaspoon dry mustard
¼ teaspoon ground ginger
1 teaspoon freshly ground black pepper
Pinch of powdered cloves

Place the beans in a colander and rinse under cold water. Pick over and discard discolored or split beans.

Transfer the beans to a large 4-quart heavy saucepan (not aluminum) and pour in enough water to cover the beans by about 3 inches. Bring to a full boil over a high heat and let boil rapidly for 2 minutes. Remove scum as it rises to the top of the water. Take the saucepan from the stove and let the beans soak in the hot water for 1 hour.

Return the pot to the stove and bring the liquid to a full boil again. Lower the heat, partially cover, and let simmer for 30 minutes.

Remove from the heat once more and drain the beans in a colander set over a large bowl, saving the cooking liquid.

Preheat oven to 250° F.

Mix the chopped onion into the beans and ladle the mixture into a 4-quart bean pot.

Rinse the salt pork under hot water and scrape the rind until white. Score the fatty side by making diagonal cuts ½ inch deep and about ½ inch apart. Put the salt pork down into the beans.

Pour 2 cups of the still-hot cooking liquid into a large bowl, add the remaining ingredients, and stir until blended and the sugar has dissolved. Pour the liquid over the beans and salt pork and with a long-handled wooden spoon, lift and mix the beans with the liquid.

Cover the pot and place it in the center of the oven and bake for 7 to 8 hours. Uncover the pot for the last half hour of cooking time.

If necessary, though it is unlikely, after about 4 hours you may add ½ to 1 cup bean cooking liquid to the pot, but remember, though the beans should be moist while cooking, very little liquid should remain when they are ready to eat.

Makes 8 to 10 servings.

SUMMER SUCCOTASH

1 cup fresh butter beans
1 small onion, peeled and chopped
½ cup chopped boiled or baked ham
1½ cups water
4 large ears fresh corn, shucked
⅓ cup heavy cream
1 tablespoon butter
Salt
Freshly ground black pepper

Place the beans in a large saucepan. Add the onion, ham, and water. Partially cover the pan and cook over a moderate heat until the beans are tender. Drain off all water.

Cut the corn kernels from the cobs and add them to the beans. Add the cream and butter and stir over a medium heat until the corn is tender and hot. Season to taste with salt and pepper and serve at once.

Makes 4 servings.

BROWN BREAD

¾ cup graham flour
1 cup white cornmeal
1 cup whole-wheat flour
1½ teaspoons baking soda
1 teaspoon salt
1 teaspoon baking powder
¾ cup seedless raisins
¾ cup chopped nuts
¼ cup stone-ground white flour
2 tablespoons white vinegar
2 cups milk, at room temperature
½ cup molasses

Sift the graham flour, cornmeal, whole-wheat flour, baking soda, salt, and baking powder into a large mixing bowl.

Mix the raisins and nuts with the white flour and add to the first mixture.

Stir the vinegar into the milk and blend. Stir into the molasses. Add the liquid mixture to the dry mixture, stirring only until blended.

Butter well 3 No. 2 cans and fill ⅔ full with the batter. Cover the tops of the cans with foil and hold in place with rubber bands. Place the cans on a rack in a steamer, fill the steamer with warm water up to ½ the height of the molds, and bring to a boiling point. Cover the steamer tightly. Lower the heat and let the water simmer for 2 hours, replenishing the water as needed to maintain the original level. Serve hot.

Makes 3 loaves.

ह≫

CRANBERRY-SAUCE CRUNCH

½ cup water
¾ cup white sugar
1 pint cranberries
¼ teaspoon cinnamon
¼ teaspoon ground cloves
1 tablespoon finely chopped lemon rind
2 cups stone-ground (slow-cooking) oatmeal
1 cup stone-ground white flour
1 teaspoon baking soda
1½ cups firmly packed brown sugar
2 tablespoons butter
Heavy cream

Combine the water, white sugar, cranberries, cinnamon, cloves, and lemon rind in a saucepan over a moderate heat. Cook, stirring often, until the sugar has melted and the cranberries pop. Remove the berries with a skimmer and let the juices boil to a thick syrup.

Pour the syrup over the berries and cool.

Preheat oven to 350° F.

Mix together the oatmeal, flour, baking soda, and brown sugar. Cut in the butter with a pastry cutter or 2 knives until crumbly.

Spread half of the mixture over the bottom of a 9 by 9-inch greased baking dish. Cover with the cooled cranberry sauce and top with the remaining mixture.

Bake for 40 to 45 minutes.

Serve warm with heavy cream over each serving.

Makes 8 to 10 servings.

NEWPORT APPLE SLUMP

2 cups stone-ground white flour

1 teaspoon salt

1 teaspoon sugar

⅓ cup butter

⅓ cup lard (or vegetable shortening)

¼ cup ice water

*10 to 12 large, crisp, tart apples, peeled, quartered, and
   cored*

¼ teaspoon nutmeg

¼ teaspoon cinnamon

3 cups molasses

Heavy cream

Preheat oven to 425° F.

Sift the flour, salt, and sugar into a large mixing bowl.
Cut in the butter and lard with a pastry cutter or 2 knives
until the mixture resembles coarse cornmeal. Sprinkle the
water, 1 tablespoon at a time, over the mixture. Mix lightly
with a fork until the mixture is moistened. With floured
hands gather the dough into a ball, turn out onto a floured
board, and roll out.

Line the bottom and sides of a deep 8-inch baking
dish with the rolled-out dough, letting the overlapping
dough hang over the sides of the dish and allowing enough
to fold over and cover the top of the dish completely.

Fill the dough-lined dish with the apples to about 1
inch of the rim. Sprinkle with the nutmeg and cinnamon
and pour the molasses over the apples. Then bring the
overlapping dough over so that the filling is completely
covered.

Place in the preheated oven and bake for 10 minutes. Reduce the heat to 325° F. and continue to bake for 30 minutes, or until the top crust is crisp and lightly browned.

Serve warm or cold, with heavy cream over each serving. Makes 8 to 10 servings.

ॐ

RHODE ISLAND BLUEBERRY SLUMP

2 cups stone-ground white flour
3 teaspoons baking powder
2 tablespoons butter
2 tablespoons vegetable shortening
¾ cup milk
1½ quarts blueberries
¾ cup sugar
½ cup water
1 tablespoon lemon juice
Heavy cream

Combine the flour and baking powder in a mixing bowl. Add the butter and shortening. Cut with a pastry cutter or 2 knives until the mixture has the consistency of corn-meal. Add the milk all at once and stir until moistened. Form into a ball, handling the dough as little as possible. Set aside.

Place the berries, sugar, water, and lemon juice in a large deep saucepan over a medium heat. When the mixture comes to a full boil, drop the dough a spoonful at a time on the fruit around the edge of the pan. Cover, reduce the heat to low, and cook 25 to 30 minutes, or until the dumplings are thoroughly cooked.

Place the dumplings in individual dessert bowls and spoon the blueberries over them.

Serve warm or cold, with the heavy cream.

Makes 8 to 10 servings.

HOREHOUND CANDY

This is an old New England bittersweet standby for winter coughs and colds.

1 tablespoon dried crumbled horehound leaves
2 cups boiling water
3 cups sugar
1 teaspoon cream of tartar
1 teaspoon butter
1 teaspoon lemon juice
Powdered sugar

Place the horehound leaves in a teapot and pour the boiling water over them, just as you would in making tea. Let stand 30 minutes and then strain through a fine sieve into a saucepan. Discard leaves.

Mix the sugar and cream of tartar and add to the horehound tea. Place over a medium heat and let come to a gentle boil, stirring until the sugar dissolves. Cook, without stirring, until the mixture reaches 200° F. on a candy thermometer. Add the butter but do not stir. Continue cooking until the thermometer reaches 325° F. Remove from the heat and stir in the lemon juice.

Pour immediately into shallow, well-buttered pans. Let cool slightly. Then, with a sharp knife, mark into small squares, deepening the marking as the candy cools.

When the candy is cold, break it into squares and roll the squares in the powdered sugar.

The candy will keep well if packed in clean, dry jars.

Makes sufficient candy to fill 3 8-ounce jars.

ε≈

SWITCHEL
(original recipe)

"For one gallon, fill the jug with ice, and pour onto the ice in the jug one cupful of molasses. Add one tablespoonful of ginger and two lemons squeezed and the rind. Or, if you do not have the lemons, use vinegar, and fill the jug with water."

ε≈

NEWPORT SWITCHEL

Switchel is the drink that seems to be most commonly associated in Rhode Island with haying time. Webster says of Switchel: "A drink made with molasses and water, sometimes with vinegar, ginger, or rum added." Switchel jugs hang in almost every old barn in the Newport area. It is a very pleasant drink for hot weather—and very old-fashioned!

4 teaspoons molasses
4 tablespoons lemon juice
4 ounces light rum
Crushed ice
Cool well water
Lemon-peel twists

Mix together the molasses, lemon juice, and rum.

Fill 4 tall glasses with crushed ice. Pour the molasses and rum mixture equally into each glass. Add a little well water to each. Garnish each with a thin twist of lemon peel.

Makes 4 servings.

NOTE: Lacking water cool from a well, use bottled mineral water—or better yet, although not authentic, use bottled Perrier water!

GREEN-TOMATO PICKLES

Early Newport housewives made good use of the products of their farms and gardens. What was not eaten during the summer months was made into a variety of pickles and relishes; and although these recipes have been adapted and changed over the years with modern cooking equipment and procedures, they still retain a flavor of those first days of the colony.

An ASTRONOMICAL DIARY : Or,

ALMANACK

For the Year of our Lord CHRIST,

1 7 6 4.

Being BISSEXTILE, or LEAP-YEAR.

Calculated for the Meridian of *Boston, New-England,* Lat. 42 Deg. 25 Min. *North.*

CONTAINING,

Eclipses ; Ephemeris ; Aspects ; Spring-Tides ; Judgment of the Weather ; Feasts and Fasts of the Church ; Courts in *Massachusetts-Bay, New-Hampshire, Connecticut,* and *Rhode-Island* ; Sun and Moon's Rising and Setting ; Time of High-Water ; Roads, with the best Stages or Houses to put up at.—A Page for Gentlemen.—On Tobacco.—On Snuff.—On good Punch.—A Page for the Husbandmen.

By *Nathaniel Ames.*

OLD Nick's a Fool, and *so bewitch'd to Sin,*
    That he 'has overshot himself again :
To set the Devil-driven Savages on us,
They'll work our Weal, though he but aim'd to curse.
They'll make a Train of nodding Virtues rise ;
And be a School to keep a People wise ;
And noble Heroes form and exercise.
    AMERICA ! thy Int'rest understood,
There are blest Omens of thy future Good :
What though the Lancit the vital Fluid spills,
It keeps the Body free from greater Ills.

NEWPORT, Rhode-Island : Re-print. and sold by
SAMUEL HALL.

The cover of an early almanac printed in Newport by Samuel Hall (*The Rhode Island Historical Society*)

Lord B. take Snuff, Mr W, and all the Journeymen and ap
prentices in London, notwithstanding they are in another way,
take Snuff also ; but besides its being fashionable to take S nuff
here is some real Advantage in it ; the Snuff, and the fine Box
which contains it, serve the Beau instead of Ideas ; when the
Jest goes round, and the Laugh is put upon him, instead of a
smart Repartee, he gravely pulls out his Box, and says—

 I am a Gentleman——and that's enough,
 Laugh if you please, I'll take a Pinch of Snuff.

 But some Ladies have taken Snuff at the Gentlemen for
using it to Excess, because it makes them appear slovenly ; and
Men of Sense affirm, that the excessive Use of it produces
Apoplexies, and Disorders arising from Obstructions of the
Animal Spirits. Thirdly,

  Of mighty Punch, allow'd by Fate,
  To drown the Pilot of the State ;
  Maudle the Gown-Man's holy Looks ;
  And make the Lawyer burn his Books ;
  Forgetful of his Patients Ills,
  Physicks the Doctor without Pills ;
  Yet Punch for Aid is still implor'd,
  And by its Votaries ador'd.
  Nectarion Dew, pure and divine,
  Belov'd by many more than Wine,
  Thou shar'd due Honours with the Vine ;
  When Wine inflames, Punch does but cheer,
  Nor fuddles like the muddy Beer ;
  But like the Fountain runs off clear.

 The Punch-Drinkers of this Day may certainly boast of a
Æra, wherein that Liquor is made more suitable to the Nature
and Constitution of Man, than the Punch which was made in
the Days of Yore. That you may know what Punch was a
Hundred Years ago, I shall give you a Receipt verbatim from
Doctor Salmon, to make a Bowl of Punch, viz.

 " Fair Water two Quarts, pure Limejuice a Pint, treble re
 " fined Sugar, 3 Quarters of a Pound, or better, mix and per
 " fectly dissolve the Sugar, then add of choice Brandy 3 Pints
 " stirring them well together, and grating in one Nutmeg."
But to make a modern Bowl of Punch a la mode ; to the above
Quantity of Water, 6 Lisbon Lemons, not quite so much Sugar,
one sixth Part of the Spirits, and the Nutmeg to be omitted.

  To the lost Wretch, who ceaseless craves the Bowl,
  Th' inebriating Draught such Pleasure gives,
  That Reason and Religion both in vain,
  Their pure and heavenly Prohibitions urge.

The almanac's tribute to punch and a charming if inadequate
recipe (*The Rhode Island Historical Society*)

29

12 medium-sized tomatoes (about 3½ pounds)
1 large cauliflower
6 medium cucumbers
5 medium onions
1 cup salt
12 cups cider vinegar
8 cups cold water
7 cups dark-brown sugar
1 tablespoon mustard seed
1 tablespoon cloves
1 tablespoon celery seed

Wash the tomatoes and cauliflower and cut into 1-inch chunks. Peel and chop the cucumbers and onions. Combine the vegetables and salt in a deep enamelized pot and cover with cold water. Stir until the salt dissolves. Cover and let stand at room temperature overnight.

Drain the vegetables and add 5 cups of the vinegar and the 8 cups of cold water. Bring to a boil and then immediately remove from the heat. Drain the vegetables and put into a deep ceramic or glass bowl. Discard the brine.

Pour the remaining 7 cups of vinegar into the pot and add the sugar, mustard seed, cloves, and celery seed. Bring to a full boil and stir until the sugar dissolves. Add the vegetables and cook over a high heat. Cook only until the vegetables are barely tender.

Pack into hot sterilized pint jars. Pour the liquid around the vegetables to cover completely. Partially seal the jars and then process them in a boiling-water bath for 15 minutes. Tighten the seal and store in a cool place.

Makes about 8 pints.

NOTE: Processing by the water-bath method is simplicity itself. Place a cake rack in the bottom of a heavy kettle deep enough to hold the jars with about 3 inches to spare. Fill the bottle with water and heat to steaming; lower the jars onto the rack and allow the water to cover the jars completely. Bring to a full rolling boil for the recommended processing time. Remove the jars from the bath, tighten the seal, cool, and store.

ટે≫

RHODE ISLAND CORN RELISH

12 cups corn kernels
6 small onions, peeled and finely chopped
3 green peppers, seeded and finely chopped
2 red bell peppers, seeded and finely chopped
2 cups brown sugar
2 tablespoons mustard seed
3 tablespoons salt
2 tablespoons celery seed
3½ cups cider vinegar

Combine all the ingredients in a deep, heavy, enamelized saucepan. Bring to a boil and cook, stirring frequently, for 15 to 20 minutes. Pour into hot sterilized pint jars, partially seal, and process in a boiling-water bath for 15 minutes. Tighten the seal and store in a cool place.

Makes about 8 pints.

Wild ducks, pheasant, squabs, venison, and quail—all exotic delicacies to us today—were the mainstay of the colonists' meals. Game is among the great pleasures of the table, and it is still, as it was in early times, wonderfully easy to prepare. Today various game may be found, ready to cook, at specialty markets—so you can put that shotgun back on the mantle!

VENISON STEAK

1 cup olive oil
1 large onion, peeled and minced
¼ cup white-wine vinegar
1 teaspoon salt
½ teaspoon pepper
6 1-inch-thick venison steaks
Butter, at room temperature
Tart jelly

Combine the olive oil, onion, vinegar, salt, and pepper. Pour over the steaks in a nonmetal pan. Let stand 1 to 2 hours at room temperature.

Drain and dry the meat thoroughly. Broil under a medium heat for 10 to 12 minutes, turning once.

Spread the steaks as they come from the broiler with soft butter.

Serve with tart jelly.

Makes 6 servings.

VENISON ROAST

Marinade:

    2 tablespoons butter
    1 tablespoon oil
    2 carrots, scraped and chopped
    1 onion, peeled and chopped
    1 celery stalk, chopped
    2 cloves garlic, peeled and minced
    1 sprig fresh rosemary
    1 sprig fresh thyme
    1 small bay leaf
    10 peppercorns
    1 teaspoon salt
    2 cups dry white wine
    2 cups water
    2 tablespoons white-wine vinegar

Roast:

    1 6- to 8-pound venison roast
    10 thin 2-inch strips salt pork
    1 tablespoon butter
    1 tablespoon flour
    2 tablespoons currant jelly
    Salt
    Pepper

Place the butter and oil in a large stew pot over a moderate heat. When the butter has melted, add the carrots, onion, celery, and garlic. Sauté until the vegetables are limp. Add the remaining marinade ingredients and bring to a full boil. Lower the heat and let simmer for 10 minutes. Remove from the heat and let cool before using.

Whitehall, one of the early Newport plantations (*Culver Pictures, Inc.*)

Make 10 deep incisions in the roast with a sharp thin pointed knife and force a strip of the salt pork into each incision.

Place the roast in a deep nonmetal bowl and pour the cooled marinade over the roast's surface. Cover and refrigerate for 12 to 24 hours, occasionally turning the meat in the marinade.

Preheat oven to 450° F.

Remove the meat from the marinade and arrange on a rack in a roasting pan.

Strain the marinade and set aside. Discard solids.

Place the meat in the preheated oven and roast: 8 minutes to the pound for rare meat, 10 minutes to the pound for medium rare.

Remove the roast to a heated platter. Remove the roasting pan from the oven and add the butter to the juices in the pan. When the butter is melted, stir in the flour and blend well, then stir in 2 cups of the strained marinade. Return the pan to the top of the stove and cook the sauce over a moderate heat until thick and smooth. Add the jelly and stir until melted. Season to taste with salt and pepper.

Slice the meat and ladle some of the sauce over each serving. Pass the remaining sauce in a sauce boat at the table.

Makes 6 to 8 servings.

ह৯

ROASTED QUAIL

6 quail
Salt
Pepper
12 teaspoons butter
2 teaspoons flour
½ cup cooking sherry
¼ cup water
¼ teaspoon marjoram

Preheat oven to 400° F.

Clean and truss the quail. Sprinkle with salt and pepper. Place 1 teaspoon of the butter in each cavity.

Mix 2 teaspoons of the butter with the flour and rub the mixture over the entire surface of each bird.

Melt the remaining 4 teaspoons of butter in a small saucepan over a moderate heat. (Do not allow to brown.) Remove the pan from the heat. Add the sherry, water, and marjoram. Set aside.

Place the quail in a roasting pan and put in the pre-heated oven. Immediately reduce the heat to 350° F. After 5 minutes start basting the birds with the butter and sherry mixture. Baste and turn the birds frequently until tender, about 1 hour.

Makes 6 servings.

QUAIL WITH PORT SAUCE

6 quail
Salt
⅓ cup butter
Port Sauce (see recipe below)

Clean and truss the quail and sprinkle with salt.

Melt the butter in a deep heavy skillet over a moderate heat. Add the quail and cook, turning and basting until lightly browned, about 15 minutes.

Cover the skillet partially and continue to cook until the birds are tender and well browned, about 15 minutes more.

Remove the birds to a heated platter and keep warm. Remove the skillet from the heat for use in making the sauce. Pour the Port Sauce over the birds when ready to serve.

Makes 6 servings.

Port Sauce

1 tablespoon butter
1 tablespoon flour
¾ cup clear fat-free chicken stock
½ cup port
1 long strip orange peel
Pinch of cinnamon
1 tablespoon currant jelly

Add the butter to the juices in the skillet used for cooking the quail and stir until melted. Sprinkle the flour over the butter and stir until blended. Slowly pour in the stock, stirring as it is added.

Return the skillet to the heat. Add the port, orange peel, and cinnamon. Cook, stirring, until the sauce is thick and smooth, then add the jelly and continue to stir until the jelly is melted.

Makes 6 servings.

RABBIT STEW

⅓ pound salt pork, diced
2 small rabbits, cleaned and cut into serving pieces
Salt
Pepper
Boiling water
1 large onion, peeled and chopped
1 pound fresh lima beans
1 cup fresh corn, cut from cob
2 medium potatoes, peeled and diced
1 cup stewed tomatoes
2 tablespoons butter
2 tablespoons flour

Place the salt pork in a deep heavy skillet over a moderate heat and cook, stirring frequently, until the pork is crisp and the bottom of the skillet is covered with rendered fat. Remove the pork with a slotted spoon, drain on paper toweling, and reserve.

Sprinkle the rabbit pieces with salt and pepper and place in the hot rendered fat in the skillet.

Cook, turning the rabbit pieces often until lightly

An early print of Newport showing its famous harbor (*Culver Pictures, Inc.*)

browned. Pour off as much fat as possible and add sufficient boiling water to completely cover the meat. Bring to a full boil, then reduce the heat. Add the onion, beans, and corn and let simmer for 30 minutes. Add the potatoes and tomatoes and continue to cook for 1 hour.

Cream the butter with the flour in a small bowl. Add a little of the hot liquid from the skillet and stir to make a paste. Stir this mixture into the stew and cook for a final 30 minutes, or until the rabbit and potatoes are "fork tender."

Ladle into soup bowls, sprinkle with the reserved pork cubes, and serve very hot.

Makes 6 servings.

ह≈

BREAD SAUCE FOR GAME

This sauce was often served in colonial days with roast chicken or game and when properly done, is delicious. The secret is in flavoring the milk before the bread is added.

1 small onion, peeled and chopped
1¼ cups milk
12 peppercorns
¾ teaspoon salt
2 cloves
1 bay leaf
Pinch of nutmeg
¾ cup fine dry bread crumbs
Heavy cream

Place the onion and milk in a saucepan and add the peppercorns, salt, cloves, bay leaf, and nutmeg. Place over a low heat and let steam without boiling for 10 to 15 minutes.

Strain the milk and return it to the saucepan, discarding solids. Bring almost to a boiling point but do not allow to boil.

Stir in the bread crumbs, then add sufficient cream to make a thin, smooth sauce. Serve very hot from a sauce boat.

Makes about 1 cup sauce.

ॐ

HOT CURRANT SAUCE FOR GAME

¼ pound butter
5 tablespoons currant jelly
2 tablespoons prepared mustard
2 teaspoons fresh lemon juice
½ cup dry sherry
½ teaspoon garlic salt
Freshly ground pepper
Salt

Place the butter in a saucepan over a very low heat. When the butter has melted, add the remaining ingredients and stir until the jelly has also melted. Cook, stirring often, until thoroughly heated. Do not allow to boil.

Serve separately with roast pheasant, Rock Cornish game hens, or any roasted game birds.

Makes about 1 cup sauce.

CHAPTER 2

"Jonny-Cake Papers"

C orn, like grapes for wine, is affected by soil and climate. The corn of Rhode Island is very different from that grown in any other locality. If you take Indian white-cap corn seed from Rhode Island and plant it in the South, the first-year corn will somewhat resemble that of Rhode Island. If you plant seed from that corn the next year, however, the corn will be the same as any other corn grown in that neighborhood, and entirely different in taste and texture from that of the parent seed grown in Rhode Island. Due to this, Indian white-cap corn cannot be grown outside of Rhode Island, and because of the peculiarities of soil and climate Rhode Island cornmeal always was and is beyond comparison.

The Newport settlers could not improve on the flavor of the corn grown by the Indians, but they did very quickly improve the methods both of growing the crop and of grinding the meal—to such an extent that cornmeal soon became one of their food staples. Windmills and then water-powered mills were erected for the sole purpose of grinding what was then called Indian meal. The invention of new dishes followed the improved grinding methods. In old letters and diaries we find references to stir-abouts, Indian pudding, Indian dumplings, toads, and many other almost-forgotten dishes; but with all the inventive genius of the settlers, they never produced a dish that could equal the one the Indians taught them to make—although they did improve and refine it—namely, the Rhode Island jonny cake.

In those days, of course, all the cooking was done before an open fireplace, and cooking was not only a work of art but an all-day job as well. To appreciate the art and labor involved, let us see how Phillis made a jonny cake. Phillis was "Shepherd Tom's" grandfather's never-to-be-forgotten, unsurpassed, now sainted, cook. In searching the birth records of the early 1700's, we find that Shepherd Tom's real name was Thomas Robinson Hazard, author, among other works, of *Jonny-Cake Papers*, in which the superiority of Phillis as a cook is fully set forth. She was beyond question the finest . . . but it is no use, Shepherd Tom used every superlative adjective known to the English language—you must seek out and read the book yourself. The following is Shepherd Tom's description of how Phillis made a jonny cake:

> Phillis, after taking from the chest her modicum of meal, proceeded to bolt it through her finest sieve, reserving the first teacupful for the special purpose of powdering fish before being fried. After sifting the meal, she proceeded to carefully knead it in a wooden tray, having first scalded it with boiling water, and added sufficient fluid, sometimes new milk, at other times pure water, to make it a proper consistency. It was then placed on a jonny-cake board about three-quarters of an inch in thickness, and well dressed on the surface with rich sweet cream to keep it from blistering when placed before the fire. The cake was next placed upright on the

An early poster honoring Thomas Hazard's sainted cook, Phillis
(*The Rhode Island Historical Society*)

The Hazard house kitchen, meticulously restored by the Newport
Preservation Society (*The Preservation Society of Newport County,
Newport, R.I.*)

hearth before a bright, green hardwood fire supported by a heart-shaped flat-iron. First the flat's front smooth surface was placed immediately against the back of the jonny-cake board to hold it in a perpendicular position before the fire until the main part of the cake was sufficiently baked, then a slanting side of the flat-iron was turned so as to support the board in a reclining position until the bottom and top extremities of the cake were in turn baked, and lastly the board was slewed round and rested partly against the handle of the flat-iron. After a time it was discovered that the flat-iron, first invented as a jonny-cake holder, was a convenient thing to iron clothes with, and has since been used for that purpose very extensively. When the jonny cake was sufficiently done on the first side, a knife was passed between it and the board, and it was dextrously turned and anointed, as before, with sweet, golden-tinged cream, previous to being again placed before the fire. Such as I have described was the process of making and baking the best article of farinaceous food that was ever partaken of by mortal man, to wit, an old-fashioned jonny cake made of white Rhode Island cornmeal, carefully and slowly ground with Rhode Island fine-grained granite stones, and baked and conscientiously turned before glowing coals of a quick green hardwood fire, on a red-oak barrelhead supported by a flat-iron.

From the latter part of this description we find an important requisite in the grinding of cornmeal: It must be "carefully and slowly ground with Rhode Island fine-grained granite stones." Phillis would use no other meal than that ground at Hammond's mill, originally Gilbert Stuart's snuff mill. Coarse-grained stones have a tendency to break the corn up with a rolling motion, producing a round meal, whereas fine-grained stones give more of a slicing motion, producing a flat meal. "Be sure and have the meal so you can feel it a little rough when you rub it through your fingers," said Phillis. Flat meal has the sweetest and best flavor. Round meal is most likely excessively heated in grinding and thereby not only is devitalized but also loses its exquisite flavor.

The millers of Rhode Island took great pride in the product of their mills, each claiming that his meal was the best. This rivalry was also shared by those having corn to grind, and they might travel many miles to go to a certain mill when there was another a stone's throw from their homes. This historical rivalry has come down the ages, and it was not many years ago that in the Rhode Island General Assembly the best part of a day was given up to a debate between a miller from South County and one from Newport County as to the relative merits of their meal and methods of baking jonny cakes.

The debate grew out of the fact that in South County they have always made *scalded-meal* jonny cakes; that is, they pour scalding water over the meal, stirring it into a thick batter, adding a little salt and sugar if desired, then frying the little cakes, about twice the size of a tablespoon, on a hot griddle. At some time in the course of human events, however, someone in Newport County invented the more delicate *milk* jonny cake. These are made by mixing the meal with cold, rich milk into a thin batter and frying the cake, thin and about 6 inches in diameter, on a hot griddle greased with bacon fat, as you would a griddle cake. If the consistency of the batter is just right, there is a fringe of delicious brown lace all around the edges.

Shepherd Tom bewailed the trend of the times when he wrote, "Since the introduction of coal fires, cooking stoves, and common schools, the making and baking of a jonny cake has become a lost art." The baking of a jonny cake on a red-oak barrelhead before an open fire, just as Phillis used to do, certainly is a lost art, yet a well-baked jonny cake of today will metamorphose the worst of morning grouches and bring a smile to the countenance and an inward feeling of satisfaction which will last all day.

"It is not easy to make a good jonny cake, for the making is a knack that must be acquired through practice and careful adherence to the best tradition of Rhode Island cooking—but the hardest part of it is getting the meal." Most of us can no longer grow our own Indian white-cap corn and take it to our favorite mill to be ground but are entirely dependent upon the name on the package. Nevertheless it is best to remember that only Indian white-cap cornmeal will make an authentic jonny cake. So insist on getting meal made from Indian white-cap corn slowly ground between carefully cut granite stones driven by a windmill or a water-wheel mill. It is still to be found if you are determined—then try the recipes to follow and don't give up until you have acquired the knack of making a real Rhode Island jonny cake.

ॐ

SCALDED-MEAL JONNY CAKES
(South County)

1 teaspoon salt
1 teaspoon molasses
1½ cups Rhode Island cornmeal
1 tablespoon butter, at room temperature
Boiling water
Milk
Butter

Place the first 4 ingredients in a bowl in the order given and pour over these enough boiling water to make a stiff dough. Beat thoroughly and let stand a few minutes while the mixture thickens. Thin down with milk to a consistency that will readily drop off the end of a spoon.

Drop on a well-greased hot griddle from a tablespoon. Cook over a low heat for 10 to 15 minutes, turning once to brown both sides lightly.

Split the hot jonny cake in half and place a large piece of butter between the halves. When the butter has melted, serve—and watch that smile of satisfaction go around the table.

Makes about 1½ dozen small cakes.

NOTE: Some use sugar instead of molasses, whereas others use no sweetening at all. Some thin down the mixture with milk that is scalding hot. An old South County recipe, instead of directing that the mixture be dropped from a spoon, says: "Dip the hands in water and mould each spoonful in balls to be flattened to a half-inch thickness on a hot greased griddle; bake nearly half an hour with occasional turning."

ટે✍

MILK JONNY CAKES
(Newport County)

½ teaspoon salt
1 teaspoon sugar
1 cup Rhode Island cornmeal
1¾ cups milk (more as needed)
Bacon fat

Put the salt, sugar, and cornmeal in a bowl. Add the milk and mix thoroughly.

Bake on a hot griddle greased with bacon fat, as you would bake griddle cakes. Since the meal keeps swelling for some time, add more milk to keep the mixture to the proper thin consistency.

Makes 12 to 14 small cakes.

NOTE: Some prefer to omit the sugar.

ह᠉

HUCKLEBERRY OR BLUEBERRY JONNY CAKES

Prepare the same as for Scalded-Meal Jonny Cakes (pages 48–49) or Milk Jonny Cakes (page 49), but first mix a liberal portion of huckleberries or blueberries into the batter.

ह᠉

SKILLET CORN BREAD
or
JONNY-CAKE-IN-THE-OVEN

3 tablespoons butter
½ cup sugar
2 eggs, lightly beaten
1¼ cups Rhode Island cornmeal
¾ cup flour
1 tablespoon baking powder
1 teaspoon salt
1 cup milk
2 teaspoons butter
Fresh butter
Dark molasses

Preheat oven to 375° F.

Cream together the 3 tablespoons butter and the sugar. Add the eggs and beat until light and fluffy.

Sift together the cornmeal, flour, baking powder, and salt. Add, alternately with the milk, to the creamed mixture.

Meanwhile, grease a 9- or 10-inch cast-iron skillet with the 2 teaspoons butter and place it in the heated oven until the butter is sizzling hot.

As soon as the batter is mixed, pour it into the hot skillet and place the skillet immediately back into the hot oven. Bake until firm and the surface is lightly browned—about 30 minutes.

Cut into wedges and serve warm with plenty of fresh butter and dark molasses.

Makes 6 to 8 servings.

ह

INDIAN PUDDING
(very old, very good recipe)

4 cups milk
1 cup Rhode Island cornmeal
2 eggs, lightly beaten
⅓ cup finely minced suet
½ cup sugar
⅔ cup light-colored molasses
¾ teaspoon salt
½ teaspoon cinnamon
¼ teaspoon ground cloves
¼ teaspoon ground ginger
⅛ teaspoon allspice
⅛ teaspoon nutmeg
Vanilla ice cream

Preheat oven to 325° F.

Bring the milk to a boil and add the cornmeal gradually, beating vigorously as it is added. Cook, stirring, over a moderate heat until the mixture begins to thicken. Remove from the heat and cool to lukewarm.

Stir in the remaining ingredients except the ice cream and blend well.

Pour into a buttered baking dish. Place in the preheated oven and bake for 2 hours.

Serve piping hot, with a scoop of vanilla ice cream in the center of each serving.

Makes 10 to 12 servings.

PHILLIS'S INDIAN PUDDING
(one of the oldest recorded recipes for Indian Pudding)

1 tablespoon butter
½ cup boiling water
2 quarts milk
2 cups fine Rhode Island stone-ground white cornmeal
¼ teaspoon salt
2 cups dark Jamaican molasses
Fresh butter

Rub the butter around the bottom and sides of a large deep cast-iron pot. Place over a moderate heat; when the butter has melted, pour in the boiling water (this prevents the milk from burning).

Add 1 quart of the milk and let it boil up to the top of the pot. Sift the meal into the pot, holding the sifter in the left hand high over the pot so that every grain is scalded. Stir constantly. Add the salt.

Remove the pot from the heat and let it stand until the mixture is cold. Then add the molasses and the remaining milk and blend well.

Pour into a buttered deep baking dish, cover, and bake at 200° F. for 10 to 12 hours.

Serve hot with plenty of fresh butter.

Makes about 10 servings.

NEWPORT SPOON BREAD

1¾ cups milk
½ cup Rhode Island cornmeal
2 teaspoons salt
1 tablespoon sugar
1½ tablespoons butter, melted
3 egg yolks, well beaten
3 egg whites

Preheat oven to 350° F.

Heat the milk in a saucepan. When the milk is just warm, add the cornmeal, salt, and sugar. Cook, stirring, until the mixture is smooth. Remove from the heat and stir in the melted butter, then the well-beaten egg yolks.

In a separate bowl beat the egg whites until stiff, then fold them gently into the cornmeal mixture.

Pour into a well-buttered baking dish and bake in the preheated oven until firm—about 45 minutes.

Makes about 8 servings.

MALBONE HOUSE VIRGINIA SPOON BREAD

1 cup white Rhode Island cornmeal
1 cup boiling water
1 tablespoon butter, very soft
½ teaspoon salt
1 egg, well beaten
1½ teaspoons baking powder
½ cup milk
Butter

Preheat oven to 375° F.

Sift the cornmeal into a mixing bowl, pour the boiling water over it, and blend. Add the butter and stir until the butter is melted. Add the salt and well-beaten egg. Blend well. Stir in the baking powder and milk.

Pour into a well-buttered deep baking dish and bake for 40 to 45 minutes.

Serve hot with butter.

Makes about 8 servings.

ॐ

TOADS

1 cup Rhode Island cornmeal
1 cup flour
1 egg, beaten
1 cup milk
2 teaspoons baking powder
2 tablespoons sugar (or ¼ cup molasses)
Oil for frying

Mix all the ingredients except the oil thoroughly in the order given and drop from a teaspoon into very hot deep oil. Fry a few at a time until lightly browned.

Drain on paper toweling and keep warm in a 200° F. oven until ready to serve.

Serve with fried fish.

Makes about 24 small Toads.

INDIAN-MEAL BANNOCK

Speed is essential in the successful preparation of this recipe, so have all your ingredients assembled before you start.

3 eggs
2 cups milk
1 cup Rhode Island cornmeal
½ teaspoon salt
1 tablespoon butter, at room temperature

Preheat oven to 375° F.

Generously grease a 2-quart baking dish with butter.

Separate the eggs. Beat the yolks in 1 bowl until frothy. In a second bowl start beating the whites.

Meanwhile, start heating the milk.

Finish beating the egg whites until they are stiff but not dry.

By this time the milk should be steamy. Take it from the heat and pour it over the cornmeal in a large bowl. Add the salt and the butter and stir until the butter has melted. Quickly stir in the egg yolks, then fold in the egg whites.

Pour into the buttered baking dish, place in the preheated oven, and bake until firm—about 30 minutes.

Makes 6 to 8 servings.

ह्र

INDIAN DUMPLING
or
STIR-ABOUT

No Newport Christmas dinner was complete without a
Stir-About.

> *2 cups boiling water*
> *1 cup Rhode Island cornmeal*
> *½ teaspoon salt*

Put the water in a skillet on the stove over a medium
heat. Gradually stir in the cornmeal. Add the salt.

Stir constantly, cooking for 10 to 15 minutes or until
thick and smooth.

Pour into a buttered mixing bowl and let stand until
firm; when the dumpling is ready to serve, unmold onto
a platter.

Makes 6 to 8 servings.

INDIAN DUMPLING IN A BAG

> *2½ cups Rhode Island cornmeal*
> *1 teaspoon salt*
> *Milk*

Mix the cornmeal and salt with milk to form a medium
dough. Tie in a cotton cloth bag that has been wrung out in

hot water and then dusted with flour. Be sure to leave room in the bag for swelling, or the bag will burst.

Hang the bag in a pot of boiling water and cook for 3 hours. Plunge the bag in cold water and remove the dumpling.

Makes 6 to 8 servings.

ट≈

RHODE ISLAND CORN PUDDING

4 cups milk
1 cup Rhode Island cornmeal
4 tablespoons butter, at room temperature
3 eggs, lightly beaten
2 tablespoons sugar
½ teaspoon salt

Preheat oven to 350° F.

In a large saucepan heat the milk to scalding. Remove the saucepan from the heat and add the remaining ingredients in the order given, blending well after each addition.

Pour the batter into a lightly buttered earthenware baking dish. Place the dish in a large pan and add sufficient hot water to the pan to come to about 1½ inches of the rim of the dish.

Place in the preheated oven and bake until the pudding is firm—about 1 hour.

Serve hot from the dish. This makes a nice accompaniment to roast chicken or duck.

Makes 6 to 8 servings.

ह‍

PARKER HOUSE CORN ROLLS

1¼ cups flour
¾ cup Rhode Island cornmeal
4 teaspoons baking powder
½ teaspoon salt
1 tablespoon sugar
2 tablespoons butter
1 egg, lightly beaten
½ cup milk
1 tablespoon butter, very cold
¼ cup milk

Preheat oven to 390° F.

Sift the flour, cornmeal, baking powder, salt, and sugar into a large mixing bowl. With your fingers, rub in the 2 tablespoons butter until the mixture looks like flakes of coarse meal.

Combine the egg with the ½ cup milk. Add this to the first mixture and mix to form a stiff dough.

Turn the dough onto a lightly floured board and roll out about ½ inch thick. Cut with a biscuit cutter. Cut the 1 tablespoon butter into slivers and place a sliver of butter on each round of dough. Fold the dough over to completely cover the butter. Brush the tops with the ¼ cup milk, place on a baking sheet, and bake for 15 minutes in the preheated oven, or until the rolls are lightly browned.

Makes about 24 rolls.

APPLE CORNMEAL PUDDING WITH WHIPPED CREAM

2 cups milk
2 cups Rhode Island cornmeal
⅛ teaspoon salt
2 eggs, lightly beaten
4 tablespoons mincemeat
½ cup molasses
4 large, tart apples, peeled, cored, and chopped
1 teaspoon baking soda dissolved in 1 tablespoon water
1 teaspoon baking powder
Sugar
Whipped cream

Preheat oven to 325° F.

Heat the milk to steaming and pour over the cornmeal in a large mixing bowl. Add the salt and eggs. Stir to a smooth batter. Mix in the remaining ingredients except the sugar and whipped cream.

Pour into a well-buttered baking dish and bake until firm—3 to 3½ hours.

Sprinkle each serving with sugar and serve with whipped cream.

Makes 8 to 10 servings.

CHAPTER 3

Colonial Newport Sets the Table

66 And at the spring, when fish comes in plentifully, they [the Indians] have meetings from several places where they exercise themselves in gaming and playing of juggling tricks, and all manner of revelles, which they delight in; so that it is admirable to behold what pastime they use of several kind, everyone striving to surpass the other."

—from *New England Caanan*, 1620

Newport, it seems, was always a very special place. There must be something in the air of this most southern seaward tip of Aquidneck Island—this isle of peace, as the red men called it. And a place of peace it proved to be for the settlers who found sanctuary upon it.

The records show that in 1639 the town was incorporated by William Coddington, judge; Jeremy Clarke, Thomas Hazard, and Henry Bull, elders; and my very own ancestor, William Dyer, town clerk. These men and

nine others had been forced to leave Massachusetts because
of their Quaker beliefs; they had walked to Providence,
where they planned to board the first available ship sailing
to Delaware—but a meeting with Roger Williams changed
their thinking. The religious tolerance then practiced in
the Rhode Island colony and Williams's influence and
friendship with the Indian owners of Aquidneck Island
caused them to decide to remain and settle on Aquidneck.

Williams guided them down Narragansett Bay by canoe
and acted as their interpreter and agent with Chief Mean-
tononi. The land was purchased for a few brass buttons
and a small measure of wampum, the white and purple
bits of quahaug shells the Indians used for money. Soon
after the price was paid, the land was cleared, and on May
16, 1639, Newport was laid out, first on paper and shortly
thereafter in fact.

Four acres were assigned for each house lot, allowing
sufficient space for both pastures and orchards. The first
houses stood around the spring that once flowed in back
of the Colony House on Washington Square, and they
spread toward the harbor and south along what is now
Thames Street. From the start the settlement was self-
governed, its political organization eventually evolving into
the town meeting. The freedom in government was matched
by an energy in commercial initiative which found its out-
let in the sea. By 1650 Newport vessels were sailing to the
West Indies, taking sheep, pork, farm produce, butter, and
cheese to be exchanged for molasses and sugar. Not long
after, the outbound cargoes included the first American
horse breed, the famous Narragansett horses from across
the bay, which were used to turn the sugar mills of the
distant islands.

By 1700 the population was 2,600, over half of whom
were Quakers. The town was led politically and econom-
ically by the wealthy merchants—"Quaker grandees of
Rhode Island." Newcomers continued to be largely En-

The steamboat joins Newport's famed sailing ships. (*Culver Pictures, Inc.*)

glish, although a community of Sephardic Jews settled there in 1654, to be followed by others, and a sprinkling of Scots and French Huguenots.

By the 1720's Newporters had greatly extended their commerce, expanded the ship-building industry, and begun making rum. They pursued new trade routes and took part in the heartless traffic in slaves. Laden with rum, Newport vessels beat their way to West Africa and exchanged the liquid cargo for the human. The next ports of call lay in the West Indies, where the slaves were sold for molasses, sugar, and cash; then they turned home. The triangular voyage to Africa and the West Indies took a year or more, depending on conditions. Freighted with sugar, the vessels also sailed from the West Indies to Holland to obtain money to pay London merchants for manufactured goods, which were sold up and down the Atlantic coast. The city remained bound to the sea; almost every Newport man over sixteen sailed before the mast at least once in his lifetime.

Sailing out of Newport's busy harbor were two hundred vessels in the foreign trade, three hundred to four hundred domestic-trade vessels, and a regular line of London packets. Between two thousand and three thousand seamen thronged the docks, which extended a mile along the harbor. There was no storage sufficient for the accumulating riches. The harvests and produce of the East and West Indies were piled along the wharves. Crates of bananas, oranges, and all the southern fruits lay in the yards of the houses, with turtles from the Bahamas, waiting to be cooked.

Prosperous Newport demanded luxuries, which took the form of beautiful furniture made by the Townsends and the Goddards, revered names in American cabinetmaking; silverware by Arnold Collins, Samuel Vernon, and others; and clocks by William Claggett. Such artists as John Smibert, Robert Feke, Samuel King, and the youthful Gilbert Stuart were kept busy with portrait commissions. New

Girls learned the housewifely arts early in colonial Newport.

public buildings were constructed, first Trinity Church

and the Colony House, which was the seat of colonial
government, both by Richard Munday; later there were
the Brick Market, Touro Synagogue, and the Redwood
Library by Peter Harrison. Colonial Newport had found
its skyline. In the same decades the city of commerce became America's first summer resort, especially favored by
West Indian and southern planters. When the philosopher
George Berkeley landed in Newport in 1729, he observed
that it already enjoyed the reputation of a watering place.

Godfrey Malbone was among the chief Newport merchants of this period. Colonel Malbone settled in the town
about the year 1700; he engaged in several successful en-
terprises, fitting out privateers in 1740, during the French
and Spanish wars with England. A rough, bold, sea-faring
man, ready to trade in slaves or rum and to send privateers
to the Spanish main, he soon acquired a large fortune.

His country house, commenced in 1744, was famous as
the finest residence in the colonies. It was built of stone,
two stories high, with a circular staircase leading to the
cupola, which alone cost the equivalent of an ordinary
farmhouse. The story of the destruction of the Malbone
house illustrates the spirit of the time. It had cost a hundred
thousand dollars, which was not a small sum of money in a
time when a man lived well upon five hundred dollars a
year. In the year 1766, as a dinner was being prepared to
which Colonel Malbone had invited the most important
residents of the island, the woodwork around the kitchen
chimney caught fire, and although the house was of Connecticut stone, the flames soon had possession. Colonel Malbone, seeing the inevitable destruction, declared that if he
must lose his house, he would not lose his dinner; and as
it was early summer, he ordered the feast to be spread out
on the lawn, where he and his guests ate their dinner by
the light of the burning house!

Colonel Robert Gibbs, another successful merchant, had

Hunter House, one of America's ten best examples of colonial
residential architecture, reflects the beauty of early Newport. (*The
Preservation Society of Newport County, Newport, R.I.*)

Afternoon tea as it was served in colonial times: Hunter House
(*The Preservation Society of Newport County, Newport, R.I.*)

a black cook, Cudjo, who was loaned to the neighbors upon their state occasions. He educated a family of cooks in Colonel Gibbs's kitchen, and epicures from every quarter were the debtors of Cudjo. Years later, Dr. James Channing, a prominent physician of the period, wrote, probably of Cudjo himself: "When I was young, the luxury of eating was carried to the greatest excess in Newport. My first notation, indeed, of glory was attached to an old black cook, whom I saw to be the most important personage in town. He belonged to the household of my uncle, and was in great demand wherever there was to be a dinner."

Vaucluse, first the residence of Samuel Elam, then of Thomas R. Hazard, was another of the fine places of that day. It was situated on the eastern side of the island, about five miles from town. The entertainments at both the Malbone house and Vaucluse—no less than those at the homes of the gentlemen of the Narragansett shore opposite—were magnificent. It was the broad English style of hospitality: abundant, loud, and doubtless somewhat coarse and rude.

Rhode Island plantation-owners of this time were aptly, if perhaps a bit critically, described by Thomas Hazard in his diary:

> This state of society, supported by slavery, produced festivities and dissipation, the natural result of wealth and leisure. Excursions to Hartford to luxuriate on bloated salmon were the annual indulgences of May. Pace races on the beach for the prize of a silver tankard, and roasts of shelled and scaled fish, were the social indulgencies of summer; when the autumn arrived, the corn-husking festivities commenced. Invitations were extended to all those proprietors who were in the habits of family intimacy, and, in return, the invited guests sent their slaves to aid the host. Expensive entertainments were prepared, and after the repast the recreation of dancing commenced, as every family was provided with a large hall in their spacious mansions, and with natural musicians among their slaves.

Gentlemen in their scarlet coats and swords, with laced ruffles over their hands, hair turned back from the forehead and curled and frizzled, clubbed or queued behind, highly powdered and pomatumed; small-clothes, silk stockings, and shoes ornamented with brilliant buckles; and ladies dressed in brocade, cushioned head-dresses, and high-heeled shoes, performed the formal minuet with its thirty-six different positions and changes. These festivities would sometimes continue for days, and the banquet among the landed proprietors would, for a longer or shorter time, be continued during the season of harvest. These seasons of hilarity and festivity were as gratifying to the slaves as to their masters, as bountiful preparations were made, and like amusements were enjoyed by them in the large kitchens and out houses.

At Christmas commenced the Holy days. The work of the season was completed and done up, and the twelve days were generally devoted to festive associations. Every gentleman of estate had his circle of connecting friends and acquaintances, and they were invited from one plantation to another.

Newport was distinguished for its frank and generous hospitality. There were few public houses. Gentlemen and strangers stayed with their friends or brought letters that secured them ample attention. The tavern of "Uncle Tom" Townsend—the Townsends of later days—was a two-story house where ardent spirits were sold, judges stopped upon the circuit, and chance travelers stayed. It is doubtless the house where the diplomat and writer Brissot de Warville lodged in 1788, and which he describes as full of travelers and sailors, whose conversation became so irksome to him that he was obliged to retreat into a small "cabinet," where he could read and write undisturbed.

From 1730 to the Revolution Newport was at the height of its prosperity. New York, New Haven, and New London greatly depended upon it for their foreign supplies. It was, indeed, a long step in time, distance, and customs from the first log-cabin settlement of Plymouth to the elegant homes of the prosperous citizens of Newport.

Early Newport Bill of Fare—1650

First Course
A Neat's Tongue and Cauliflowers
A Forequarter of Lamb
A Chicken Pie
Boylee Pigeons with New Peas*
A Couple of Stewed Rabbits
A Breast of Veal Roasted
Second Course
An Artichoke Pie
A Venison Pastry
Lobsters and Salmon
A Gooseberry Tart
A Dish of Strawberries

A Malbone House Dinner—1740

Oysters on the Half Shell
Turtle Soup
Poached Salmon with Rich Cream Sauce
and Steamed New Potatoes and Fresh Peas*
A Grand Salad of Watercresses
Wild Duck from the Spit
Bread Sauce
A Salamagundy with Meats
Plum Pudding with Rum Sauce
Strawberry Truffle
Cheese and Pipins

* Recipe follows.

New Year's Breakfast at Vaucluse

Brook Trout   Poached Salmon
Fried Eggs   Baked Eggs in Cream
Sausage Cakes   Bacon
Grilled Pheasant
Roasted Quail
Cold Smoked Ham   Braised Turkey Pie
Apple Jelly   Quince Jelly
Hot Rolls
Hothouse Peaches, Nectarines, and Grapes

A Typical Newport Christmas Dinner

Roast Beef   Roast Pork
Roast Turkey with Corn-Bread and Oyster Stuffing*
Roast Goose with Chestnut-Apple Stuffing†
Boiled Mashed Turnips   Creamed Onions
Baked Winter Squash   Winter Succotash
Celery   Cranberry Sauce   Cucumber Pickles
Plum Cake
Rum Pumpkin Meringue Pie†
Raisins   Apples   Nuts   Oranges
Christmas Punch

High Tea at Vaucluse

Sweet Mincemeat Tea Biscuits†
Tea Bread†
English High-Tea Gingerbread†
Catherine Ray Quick Cake†
Fresh Butter   Quince Jam
Tea with Milk and Sugar

* See pages 15–18.
† Recipe follows.

America's gracious heritage epitomized by a table setting of impeccable taste: Hunter House (*The Preservation Society of Newport County, Newport, R.I.*)

BOYLEE PIGEONS WITH NEW PEAS

This is a decidedly old English dish brought to this country but little changed. In the adaptation below, tender little squabs (pigeons before they fly), especially raised for the market, are used, but the method of cooking the remaining ingredients stands as written in the eighteenth century.

½ cup chopped celery
½ cup chopped onion
1 tablespoon chopped parsley
1 tablespoon butter
2 cups crumbled unsalted cracker crumbs
1 sprig minced fresh thyme
Pinch of mace
Pinch of nutmeg
½ teaspoon grated lemon peel
1 large egg, beaten
Salt
Pepper
6 squabs, ready for stuffing
2 tablespoons butter
½ pound chopped mushrooms
1 tablespoon flour
1 cup clear, fat-free chicken stock
½ cup Madeira
1 teaspoon Worcestershire sauce
1 teaspoon lemon juice
3 cups freshly cooked new green peas

Preheat oven to 375° F.

Sauté the celery, onion, and parsley in the 1 tablespoon butter until limp. Remove from the heat and stir in the cracker crumbs, thyme, mace, nutmeg, lemon peel, and egg. Blend well. Add salt and pepper to taste.

Sprinkle the insides of the squabs with salt and stuff them with the mixture.

Truss the squabs: Fold the wing tips back under the bird. Take a length of twine and tie the legs securely together at the ends. Make a tight loop around the tail. Then cross the string over the body and bring across the wings to hold them close to the body. Make a last loop and tie the neck skin.

Melt the 2 tablespoons butter in a large skillet (one that may be used in the oven). Add the mushrooms and cook over a low heat for about 10 minutes. Remove the mushrooms with a slotted spoon and set aside. Increase the heat to moderately high and place the squabs in the skillet, breast downward at first. Turn and brown them on all sides. Remove the squabs and set aside.

Stir the flour into the pan juices and cook, stirring, until lightly browned. Slowly add the chicken stock and Madeira and stir until the mixture is smooth. Return the squabs and mushrooms to the skillet. Cover and place in the preheated oven. Bake until the squabs are tender—about 35 minutes.

Remove the squabs to a heated platter. Place the skillet on the stove over a medium heat and reduce the sauce to half its original volume. Season with the Worcestershire sauce and lemon juice. Add the peas and mix.

Ladle the peas and sauce around the squabs and serve at once while very hot.

Makes 6 servings.

General George Washington was received here: the spacious hall at Hunter House. (*The Preservation Society of Newport County, Newport, R.I.*)

ह๑

POACHED SALMON WITH RICH CREAM SAUCE AND STEAMED NEW POTATOES AND FRESH PEAS

2 cups water
1 cup dry white wine
2 tablespoons lemon juice
1 small white onion, peeled and sliced
1 teaspoon dill seeds
1 teaspoon salt
¼ teaspoon peppercorns
4 8-ounce salmon steaks, about 1 inch thick
Rich Cream Sauce (see page 77)
1 hard-cooked egg, sliced
Chopped parsley
Steamed New Potatoes and Fresh Peas (see pages 77–78)

Combine the water, wine, and lemon juice in a deep 9-inch or 10-inch skillet. Add the onion, dill seeds, salt, and peppercorns. Let simmer for 30 to 45 minutes. Add the salmon steaks. Cover and poach for 15 minutes, or until the salmon flakes easily when tested with a fork.

Remove the salmon with a spatula. Let drain over the skillet, then place on a warm serving platter or on warm plates. Keep warm.

Strain the cooking liquid and reserve 2 cups for the Rich Cream Sauce.

When ready to serve, ladle the Rich Cream Sauce over the salmon steaks and garnish each serving with the egg slices and chopped parsley. Surround with the Steamed New Potatoes and Fresh Peas.

Makes 4 servings.

Rich Cream Sauce

2 tablespoons butter
2 tablespoons flour
*2 cups strained salmon cooking liquid (see recipe for
   Poached Salmon)*
2 egg yolks, lightly beaten
½ cup light cream
Salt
Freshly ground white pepper
1 teaspoon lemon juice

Melt the butter in a saucepan (not aluminum) and stir in the flour. Slowly add the strained cooking liquid, stirring with a wire wisk as it is added. Bring to a boil and cook, stirring often, for about 5 minutes. Remove from the heat.

Beat the egg yolks into the cream and add this to the first mixture, beating constantly with a wire wisk. Return the mixture to a low heat and stir until thick and smooth. Season to taste with salt and pepper. Remove from the heat and stir in the lemon juice.

Makes 4 servings.

Steamed New Potatoes and Fresh Peas

12 very small new potatoes (about 1½ pounds)
1 teaspoon salt
3 tablespoons butter
⅓ cup water
2 pounds shelled fresh peas

Wash and scrape the potatoes. Place them in a saucepan. Add the salt, butter, and water. Cover and let steam over a moderate heat for 10 minutes. Shake the pan oc-casionally and tilt it back and forth. Resist the temptation to uncover the pan. Steam is your cooking method, so as little as possible should be allowed to escape.

Add the peas, re-cover the pan, and let steam until the potatoes and peas are tender—about 30 minutes.

Makes 4 servings.

ॐ

ROAST GOOSE WITH CHESTNUT-APPLE STUFFING

1 10- to 12-pound goose
Chestnut-Apple Stuffing (see page 79)

Preheat oven to 450° F.

Wash the goose, inside and out. Remove and discard all large pieces of interior fat.

Stuff the goose lightly with the Chestnut-Apple Stuffing. Skewer the opening or tie with string. Place any remaining stuffing in a buttered baking dish and bake separately.

Place the goose on a rack in an uncovered pan and roast in the preheated oven for 20 minutes. Reduce the heat to 350° F. Continue to cook for a total of 30 minutes for each pound or until well browned and crisp and the drumsticks move up and down easily.

Spoon out the fat as it accumulates.

Makes 6 to 8 servings.

Chestnut-Apple Stuffing

¾ cup butter

1 large onion, peeled and diced

1 1-pound loaf 2- or 3-day-old white bread, cut into cubes

1½ cups chicken stock (or broth)

½ cup calvados (or applejack)

2 teaspoons salt

½ teaspoon pepper

2 cups diced, peeled, and cored apples

1 cup chestnuts, toasted and chopped

Preheat oven to 350° F.

Melt the butter in a large frying pan. Add the onion and sauté until limp.

Remove from the heat and add the bread cubes. Toss and stir until the cubes are coated with the butter. Turn out on foil and place in the preheated oven until lightly browned.

Place in a large mixing bowl and add the remaining ingredients. Blend well.

Makes 6 to 8 servings.

ßℴ

RUM PUMPKIN MERINGUE PIE

1 unbaked pie pastry crust
3 egg yolks, lightly beaten
¼ cup molasses
¾ cup sugar
½ teaspoon salt
½ teaspoon ground ginger
½ teaspoon ground nutmeg
¼ teaspoon cinnamon
1 cup light cream
2 cups mashed cooked pumpkin pulp
¼ cup dark rum
3 egg whites
¼ teaspoon cream of tartar
¼ teaspoon salt
⅓ cup sugar
1 tablespoon dark rum

Preheat oven to 425° F.

Line a 9-inch pie plate with the pastry.

Combine the egg yolks, molasses, and ¾ cup sugar. Beat with a wire wisk until the sugar has dissolved. Add the ½ teaspoon salt and the ginger, nutmeg, cinnamon, and cream. Blend and add the pumpkin a little at a time, mixing well after each addition. Stir in the ¼ cup rum.

Pour the mixture into the prepared pie shell, place in the preheated oven, and bake for 15 minutes. Lower the heat to 350° F. and continue to bake until the filling is firm—about 30 minutes.

Remove the pie from the oven and let stand at room temperature until cool.

Preheat oven to 350° F.

Beat the egg whites until frothy. Add the cream of tartar and the ¼ teaspoon salt and continue to beat until stiff but not dry. Beat in the ⅓ cup sugar a little at a time, beating well after each addition. Fold in the 1 tablespoon rum.

Spread the meringue evenly over the entire surface of the pie to the edge of the shell. Pull the meringue up into peaks.

Return the pie to the preheated oven and bake until the meringue is delicately browned—about 15 minutes.

Makes 1 9-inch pie.

ટ≈

SWEET MINCEMEAT TEA BISCUITS

1 9-ounce package mincemeat
3 tablespoons water
½ cup (1 stick) butter, soft
⅓ cup shortening
1½ cups sugar
3 eggs, well beaten
3 cups flour
1 cup chopped walnuts
1 teaspoon baking soda
½ teaspoon nutmeg

Preheat oven to 375° F.

Place the mincemeat in a small bowl, add the water, blend, and set aside.

In a large mixing bowl cream the butter and shortening with the sugar. Add the eggs and beat well.

Add 1½ cups of the flour to the butter mixture and blend to smooth the batter. Stir in the mincemeat. Mix the remaining 1½ cups flour with the walnuts, baking soda, and nutmeg. Add to the batter and blend.

Drop by spoonfuls onto a greased and floured baking sheet. Bake in the preheated oven until firm—about 10 minutes.

Makes about 36 small biscuits.

ટે

TEA BREAD
or
NEW ENGLAND RAISED CAKE

1 cup milk
1 1-ounce package granular yeast
¼ cup sugar
1 cup flour
½ pound butter
1¾ cups sugar
2 cups flour
1 egg, lightly beaten
1 teaspoon grated lemon rind
¼ teaspoon nutmeg
1 teaspoon salt
¾ cup seedless raisins
1 cup chopped citron
½ cup chopped maraschino cherries

Scald the milk. Cool to lukewarm. Add to the yeast in a large mixing bowl and blend well. Add the ¼ cup sugar and the 1 cup flour.

Cover with a clean cloth and let rise in a warm place until foamy—about 1 hour.

Cream the butter with the 1¾ cups sugar and add to

the first mixture alternately with the 2 cups flour and the egg. Fold in the remaining ingredients. Put into 2 well-buttered bread pans, filling each about half full. Let stand at room temperature for 2 hours.

Preheat oven to 350° F.

Bake in the preheated oven for 15 minutes. Lower the temperature to 300° F. and continue to bake for 50 to 60 minutes, or until the cakes are firm and lightly browned. Turn out onto racks to cool.

Because of the butter content, the cakes will rise only slightly.

Makes 2 loaves.

NOTE: The cakes may be returned to the cleaned bread pans, covered with foil, and stored for 2 to 3 weeks.

ह

ENGLISH HIGH-TEA GINGERBREAD

4 tablespoons corn syrup
½ cup firmly packed light-brown sugar
¼ pound butter, at room temperature
1 tablespoon lard (or vegetable shortening)
1 egg, well beaten
½ cup milk
2 cups flour
½ teaspoon ground ginger
1 teaspoon baking powder
⅓ cup chopped crystallized ginger
½ cup chopped almonds

Preheat oven to 350° F.

Combine the corn syrup and sugar. Add the butter and lard. Beat until well blended.

Combine the egg with the milk and add to the sugar mixture alternately with the flour. Beat well. Add the ground ginger and baking powder. Blend and then fold in the chopped ginger and almonds.

Pour into a well-buttered and floured square baking pan and bake until firm—about 40 minutes.

Cool and cut into squares.

Makes 8 to 10 small squares.

ॐ

CATHERINE RAY QUICK CAKE

¼ cup flour
½ cup raisins
3¾ cups flour
2 teaspoons cream of tartar
2 egg yolks
1 cup milk
1 teaspoon baking soda
2 egg whites
½ cup melted butter

Preheat oven to 425° F.

Add the ¼ cup flour to the raisins, mix together, and set aside.

Sift the 3¾ cups flour with the cream of tartar into a mixing bowl.

Beat the egg yolks until light, add ½ cup of the milk, and blend well. Set aside.

Add the baking soda to the remaining ½ cup milk and blend well. Set aside.

Beat the egg whites until stiff.

To the flour and cream of tartar add the egg and milk

mixture and mix well. Add the milk and baking-soda mixture and again beat well. Fold in the beaten egg whites, then the melted butter, and lastly the floured raisins.

Pour the batter into a well-greased 10-inch cast-iron skillet and bake in the preheated oven until firm.

Makes 8 medium-sized wedges.

PART II

Of Cottages and Kings

Newport's famed Ocean House at the height of its glory (*The Rhode Island Historical Society*)

CHAPTER 4

Maude Elliott's Newport

Newport's first resorters were southern planters and their families escaping the torpid southern summer. The Newport climate lured literally hundreds of vacationers. Boardinghouses were at first the only accommodations, but as the need for more luxurious quarters became apparent, enterprising Newporters began opening hotels. There were a number of them: the Bellevue, the Whitfield, the Perry, and Cliff House. Only one was to become really famous, however—Ocean House. This huge yellow monstrosity opened in 1845 to house those early visitors in a splendor that rivaled the glitter of the Grand Union Hotel at Saratoga, New York.

The southerners were quickly followed by the Bostonians—first the substantial families and then a coterie of artists, writers, professors, and philosophers which reads like a Who's Who of the nineteenth century. Henry James, Edwin Booth, Oscar Wilde, Bret Harte, Julia Howe, and Samuel Gridley Howe were only a few of the regulars.

Julia Ward Howe's daughter, Maude Elliott, relates in her book, *This Was My Newport*, how her parents would establish themselves at the old Cliff House each summer along with such a dazzling group of literary lights that Count Gurowski, an exiled Pole, rechristened Cliff House "Hôtel Rambouillet" after the famous house of France's queen of intellectuals, Madame de Sévigné. Nevertheless, Newport's summer visitors soon tired of hotel life. A place of their own was what was wanted, and rambling, comfortable houses in the early Victorian style began to rise up in numbers. Newport's cottage era had begun.

The Howe cottage, Lawton Valley, was six miles outside Newport, but it was very much a Newport "cottage," and it seems to have been Julia Howe's favorite house. Her daughter describes their arrival for yet another summer "in a cloud-burst of rain" to be met by "Mr. Anthony," an ancient hack driver who matched her mother's "joy of actually having returned to Newport" with "the warmth of his welcome." Lawton Valley adjoined Vaucluse—the Thomas Hazard estate, with its beautiful white-columned house—and Maude Elliott captured the spirit of those early resort days with her description of afternoon tea at Vaucluse:

> The gong rang. The children, forgetting their fatigue, scrambled for the house and soon they were seated at the long mahogany table that stretched the length of that vast dining room. We knew that when there was no company, the long table came apart into a series of small tables that stood against the wall in the hall which ran through the middle of the house. We knew that its polish came from endless rubbing with cork and sweet oil—a labor of love, like all the rest of the household tasks performed by the blooming Hazard daughters. You could see your spoon reflected in that board!
>
> First we had bread and butter—airily thin the bread was cut, and the butter was "Vaucluse's" own matchless brand.

Julia Ward Howe

Then jonny cakes, fried to a delicate brown never surpassed and only rarely equaled at Miss Ruth Durfee's tea house on the Glen Road. The yellow and green pineapple in the middle of the table miraculously opened, and there was the perfect condiment for jonny cakes—granulated sugar mixed with powdered cinnamon. How fast the piles of hot cakes vanished: how regularly fresh plates of them appeared!

"Keep a place for the peaches," a wise child warned the others.

The peaches were sliced and served in cut glass saucers, eaten with thin old silver teaspoons that had come into the family with "the Robinson blood" generations ago. At the head of the feast sat Mr. Hazard—a big man with a loud voice, great bony hands, huge joints, strong heavy features, light blond hair in tight little rings, and blue eyes—the eyes of a mystic.

"Have some cherry bounce, Mrs. Howe?" he booms out in his great voice, and Mrs. Howe agreeing, a small exquisite decanter and quaint tiny glasses are produced, and the elders drink each other's health at the head of the board, while the children's silver mugs are refilled with milk.

High tea was the last meal of the day—unless you counted the midnight suppers that followed those first musicals and balls. Dinner was the main attraction. It was served at noon or one o'clock, which was just as well, for they were lengthy dinners indeed: eight to ten courses, fish, roasts, entrées, half a dozen vegetables, salads, fruits, cheeses, desserts, bonbons, and finally, coffee.

The competition for being a good host or hostess had already begun. Mrs. Howe wrote to a friend upon the occasion of Oscar Wilde's impending visit: "The house is all slicked up, uncommon, all the women have worked with a will, and Mrs. Richard Hunt's cook has made for me a pound cake with a sunflower in the middle, composed of lemon peel and angelica." It remained for the coming of Mrs. August Belmont, however, to transform the "charming country place" into an elegant and fashionable resort.

Mrs. Belmont had refined French manners, beautiful jewels, a stable of fine horses, and above all, she was a prime resorter. Dinner gave way to luncheon at midday and became the formal eight o'clock ten-course meal. Afternoon tea was served at five; there was barely time to stuff oneself into the full-dress regalia of the evening when dinner was served. Not every Newporter was delighted—"We were at the table three mortal hours," Maude Elliott reported to a friend—but like it or not, "the plain living and high thinking" of Maude Elliott's childhood was fast fading before the brilliant lights of emerging Newport society. The future queen of resorts had become a princess.

Menus from Newport's early hotels reflect a lavish hand. Anyone who could eat his way through even part of one of these meals really possessed a trencherman's appetite. Soup, boiled meat, a roast, and cold meats were the tidbits offered before the entrée! And the entrée was no trifle: The menu at Perry House listed beefsteak pie, with a choice of macaroni and cheese, asparagus, spinach, boiled rice, and turnips; the whole was seasoned with mustard, two kinds of catsup, and an assortment of relishes, pickles, olives, and sauces. For those who could continue there was apple pudding with hard sauce, followed by fresh fruit, and then —and only then—was dessert served: Charlotte Russe billowing with whipped cream. If you were still famished, there were at least six kinds of nuts offered, with raisins and crackers with cheese.

Though it is doubtful that anyone wants to duplicate a menu like this, here are the pertinent recipes—a week's worth of cooking for any family! You can, however, easily adapt the menu to modern proportions. The Newport Fish Chowder, followed by a salad and the Perry House Apple Pudding, would make a wonderful lunch or a Sunday-night supper. The Baked Codfish, rice, and spinach would make still another meal; or the Smoked Beef Tongue with Raisin

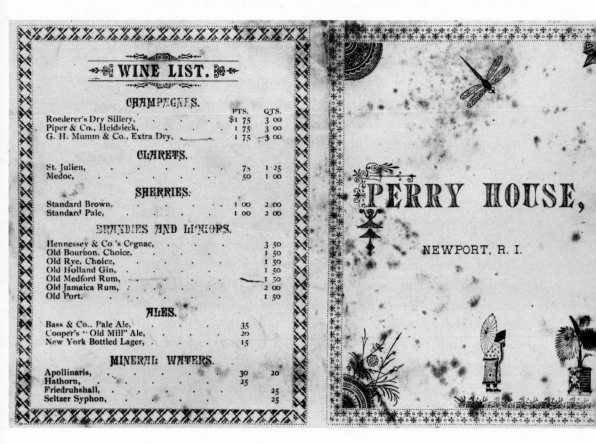

WINE LIST.

CHAMPAGNES.

	PTS.	QTS.
Roederer's Dry Sillery,	$1 75	3 00
Piper & Co., Heidsieck,	1 75	3 00
G. H. Mumm & Co., Extra Dry,	1 75	3 00

CLARETS.

| St. Julien, | 75 | 1 25 |
| Medoc, | 50 | 1 00 |

SHERRIES.

| Standard Brown, | 1 00 | 2 00 |
| Standard Pale, | 1 00 | 2 00 |

BRANDIES AND LIQUORS.

Hennessey & Co.'s Cognac,		3 50
Old Bourbon, Choice,		1 50
Old Rye, Choice,		1 50
Old Holland Gin,		1 50
Old Medford Rum,		1 50
Old Jamaica Rum,		2 00
Old Port,		1 50

ALES.

Bass & Co., Pale Ale,	35
Cooper's "Old Mill" Ale,	20
New York Bottled Lager,	15

MINERAL WATERS.

Apollinaris,	30	20
Hathorn,	25	
Friedruhshall,		25
Seltzer Syphon,		25

PERRY HOUSE,

NEWPORT, R. I.

Champagne flowed like water at $3.00 a quart, and claret sold for $1.25: Perry House menu cover. (*The Rhode Island Historical Society*)

94

Table D'Hote.

June 1st 1883

SOUP.

Fish Chowder

FISH.

Baked Cod

BOILED.

Beef Tongues

ROAST.

Chicken, Sirloin Beef
Pork apple sauce

COLD MEATS.

Roast Beef,   Corned Beef,   Ham.   Tongue,

ENTREES.

Beef Steak Pie
Baked Macaroni with Cheese

VEGETABLES.

Asparagus   *Spinach*

Boiled Potatoes,   Corn,   Beets,   Tomatoes
Mashed Potatoes,   Onions,   Beans,

Boiled Rice.   *Turnips*

RELISHES.

Pickles,   Worcestershire Sauce,   Tomato Catsup,
Celery-Salt,   Olives,   Walnut Catsup,   French Mustard.

PASTRY.

Apple Pudding — Hard sauce
Washington Apple and Blueberry Pie

DESSERT.

Charlotte Russe

Walnuts,   Brazil Nuts,   Almonds,   Filberts,
Pecan Nuts,   Raisins.

TEA.   CRACKERS AND CHEESE.   COFFEE.

Soup, fish, and roasts preceded the entrée, and pastry was served before dessert: Perry House menu, 1883. (*The Rhode Island Historical Society*)

95

Sauce, served with asparagus and macaroni and cheese; or the Pork with Horseradish Applesauce, accompanied by mashed turnips. The Beefsteak Pie would need only a crisp salad, and of course, the Charlotte Russe makes a creamily good ending anytime.

℞

NEWPORT FISH CHOWDER

½ pound salt pork, diced
2 medium onions, thinly sliced
1 4- to 4½-pound cod or haddock fillet
4 cups water
6 medium potatoes, peeled and sliced
¼ teaspoon black pepper
¼ teaspoon cayenne pepper
4 cups milk, scalded
1 cup light cream

Fry the pork over a medium heat in a deep, heavy soup kettle until all fat is rendered and the diced cubes are crisp. Remove with a slotted spoon, drain, and reserve.

Add the onion slices to the fat remaining in the kettle and fry over a low heat until golden. Cut the fillet into 2-inch pieces and add with the water to the onions. Add the potatoes, black pepper, and cayenne pepper. Cook over a low heat for 15 to 20 minutes, or until the potatoes are soft. Add the milk and continue to cook over a very low heat for an additional 10 minutes.

Stir in the cream and cook only until steamy hot. Do not allow to boil. Sprinkle in the pork cubes.

Makes 8 servings.

BAKED CODFISH

2 pounds salted codfish
4 cups water
3 tablespoons butter
3 tablespoons flour
1 cup milk, scalded
1 egg yolk, beaten
¼ teaspoon pepper
¼ cup fine dry bread crumbs
2 tablespoons chopped parsley

Soak the codfish in the water overnight.

Drain and cover with fresh water in a heavy enamelized soup kettle. Cook over a medium heat for 10 to 15 minutes until the fish is tender and flakes easily with a fork. Drain and set aside, reserving ½ cup of the liquid for the sauce.

Melt the butter in a heavy saucepan and stir in the flour. Cook for 1 to 2 minutes over a very low heat. Stir in the still-hot milk and the ½ cup of fish liquid. Continue to cook, stirring constantly, until the sauce begins to thicken. Mix about 2 tablespoons of the hot sauce with the beaten egg yolk and stir into the sauce. Add the pepper. Blend well. Remove from the heat.

Cut the codfish into bite-sized pieces and arrange in a shallow baking dish, pour the sauce over the fish, sprinkle evenly with the bread crumbs, and bake in a moderate (350° F.) oven for 20 to 25 minutes.

Sprinkle with the parsley and serve.

Makes 6 to 8 servings.

ह≫

SMOKED BEEF TONGUE WITH RAISIN SAUCE

2½ to 3 pounds smoked beef tongue
4 bay leaves
1 whole peppercorn
1 teaspoon cloves
½ teaspoon salt
1 medium onion, cut in quarters
Raisin Sauce (see recipe below)

Wash the tongue and place in a heavy enamelized soup kettle. Cover with cold water and add the remaining ingredients. Cover and simmer over a low heat for 3 to 5 hours or until tender (when the bone moves easily).

Let cool in the stock. Remove the skin and cut into uniform slices into a shallow baking dish. Set aside and make the Raisin Sauce.

Pour the Raisin Sauce over the tongue slices and place in a moderate oven (350° F.) for 10 to 15 minutes until the meat is thoroughly heated.

Makes 8 servings.

Raisin Sauce

3 tablespoons butter
1½ tablespoons flour
1 cup beef stock (or beef consommé)
2 tablespoons dry sherry
Grated rind of 1 lemon
1 cup seedless raisins

Melt the butter in a heavy saucepan and stir in the flour. Cook over a very low heat, stirring constantly, until the flour turns golden and gives off a nutty aroma—about 5 to 10 minutes.

Add the stock slowly, stirring constantly, to blend. Cook over a low heat until the sauce has thickened. Stir in the sherry, lemon rind, and raisins.

Makes 8 servings.

ಶಿ

PORK WITH HORSERADISH APPLESAUCE

1 3½- to 4-pound pork loin roast
¼ teaspoon black pepper
1½ cups beef or veal stock
2 tablespoons chopped parsley
1 bay leaf
Horseradish Applesauce (see page 100)

Preheat oven to 450° F.

Have the roast at room temperature and place on a rack in a deep heavy casserole. Roast for 20 minutes to the pound. The surface should be evenly browned. Remove the roast and keep hot.

Pour off the accumulated fat from the pan, return the meat, and pour in the beef or veal stock. Add the parsley and bay leaf. Cover tightly and cook an additional 20 minutes to the pound.

The meat should be thoroughly done, not pink. This method permits thorough cooking without dryness.

Serve with the Horseradish Applesauce.

Makes 6 to 8 servings.

Horseradish Applesauce

6 medium-sized tart apples
½ cup water
½ cup sugar
2 teaspoons prepared horseradish

Peel and core the apples; slice thinly. Place in a heavy saucepan and add the water and sugar. Cook, stirring frequently, over a moderate heat, until the apples are tender.

Break up with a spoon to form a smooth sauce. Stir in the horseradish and serve warm.

Makes 6 to 8 servings.

ॐ

BEEFSTEAK PIE

¼ pound salt pork, diced
2½ to 3 pounds beef sirloin, cut into 2-inch cubes
10 to 12 very small white onions, peeled
2 tablespoons flour
1½ cups beef stock
4 medium carrots, scraped and cut into 1-inch pieces
1 tablespoon Worcestershire sauce
¼ teaspoon salt
¼ teaspoon pepper
2 tablespoons chopped parsley
Flaky Pastry (see page 101)

Preheat oven to 450° F.
Fry the diced pork over a medium heat until crisp

and golden brown. Remove with a slotted spoon, drain, and reserve.

Heat the remaining fat until it is almost smoking. Brown the sirloin cubes in the fat a few at a time, removing to a heated casserole as they are browned.

When the meat is all browned, lower the heat and add the onions. Brown, turning frequently, until light golden. Add the onions to the meat in the casserole.

Pour off all but about 2 tablespoons of the fat. Add the flour and cook over a low heat, stirring constantly, until the flour is golden in color. Add the beef stock and cook, stirring frequently, until the sauce has thickened slightly. Pour over the meat and onions.

Stir in the carrots, Worcestershire sauce, salt, pepper, reserved pork cubes, and parsley. Cover with the Flaky Pastry and bake in the preheated oven for 10 minutes. Lower the heat to 300° F. and bake for 1 hour.

Makes 8 servings.

Flaky Pastry

*1 cup flour
¼ teaspoon salt
¼ cup butter
Ice water*

All the ingredients should be ice cold.

Sift the flour with the salt. Cut the butter into slivers and blend into the flour with a pastry blender until the mixture resembles fine meal. Chill for 1 hour.

Add ice water, a few drops at a time, until the mixture holds together. Chill again.

Roll out on a floured board and cut into a circle to fit the casserole.

Makes 1 top crust.

ð

PERRY HOUSE APPLE PUDDING

*12 to 14 soda crackers, broken into small pieces to make
  2 cups
1 cup brown sugar
½ teaspoon cinnamon
½ teaspoon allspice
8 to 10 medium-sized tart apples
3 tablespoons butter
Hard Sauce (see recipe below)*

Preheat oven to 300° F.

Combine the cracker pieces, brown sugar, cinnamon, and allspice. Peel and core the apples and slice thin.

Place a layer of the apples in an oven-proof casserole and sprinkle with a layer of the cracker-sugar mixture. Repeat layering until all the ingredients have been used, finishing with a layer of the crackers and sugar.

Dot with the butter and bake in the preheated oven for 45 to 50 minutes.

Serve warm with the Hard Sauce.

Makes 6 to 8 servings.

Hard Sauce

*1 cup confectioners' sugar
½ cup butter
2 tablespoons cognac
2 tablespoons grated lemon rind*

Cream the sugar and butter together. Beat in the cognac and lemon rind. Chill until firm.

Makes about 1¾ cups sauce.

CHARLOTTE RUSSE

16 to 20 ladyfingers
½ cup cognac
6 egg yolks
1 cup sugar
3 cups milk
1 pint heavy cream
8 to 10 maraschino cherries

Place the ladyfingers in a nonmetal shallow dish and sprinkle with the cognac. Chill.

Beat the egg yolks until light, add the sugar, and beat until well blended. Stir in the milk, pour into a heavy saucepan, and cook over a very low heat, stirring constantly, until the custard begins to thicken. Chill 4 to 6 hours or overnight.

Beat the cream until quite stiff and fold into the cold custard.

Line 8 to 10 individual serving dishes with the ladyfingers and pour the custard over them. Garnish with a maraschino cherry and serve cold.

Makes 8 to 10 servings.

From *This Was My Newport*:

The balls at Miramar, the Hamilton Rice estate, are perfect summer night entertainments. The lawn stretching down to the sea is converted into an outdoor salon; the terrace where the tables are spread, into an open air dining room. Guests are invited for half-past ten; at eleven a few admirals, the clergy, and certain elderly diehards arrive and keep the host and hostess company until the party really begins. There have been innumerable dinners before the dance, and the diners linger over their coffee and cigarettes—even play a rubber of bridge—before beginning the serious business of dancing the night through. By midnight the ball is well started. Supper is served before one o'clock for the elderly, who take from the sumptuous feast a glass of champagne punch and a roll, and then depart—leaving the ballroom clear for the real revelers, who dance until daylight, when the band plays "Home, Sweet Home." They are served with a breakfast of scrambled eggs and sausages before they leave. The youngsters with the greatest staying powers top off with a swim at Bailey's Beach before going to bed to sleep off the after-effects of the all-night festivity. The evenings of the full moon are the most popular for these summer balls, and the hostesses, in order to secure the desired night, send out their cards a month in advance.

ટ&

MIDSUMMER NIGHT'S CHAMPAGNE PUNCH

12 bottles of dry California white wine
4 cups cognac
Juice from 8 oranges
Juice from 12 lemons
Juice from 3 limes
1 cup sugar
12 bottles of champagne (chilled)
2 pints strawberries, hulled and sliced

Combine the wine, cognac, fruit juices, and sugar. Blend well and chill thoroughly.

When ready to serve, pour over a cake of ice in a punch

A ball at Newport: They could (and did) dance all night. (*The Rhode Island Historical Society*)

bowl. Add the champagne and strawberries and serve. Makes 100 servings.

NOTE: If desired, this can be prepared in smaller portions; to 8 cups of base add ⅕ gallon of champagne. Fresh punch can be mixed as needed to prevent it from becoming watery.

From *O. C. Marsh: Pioneer in Paleontology,* by Charles Schuchert and Clara Mae Le Verne:

> In August Marsh and his cousin, George Peabody Russell, went to Newport to attend the Fête Champêtre given for Mr. Peabody by Mr. William Shepard Wetmore, and [Marsh's] diary speaks of the event as "probably the greatest affair of the kind ever given in this country. Over 10,000 guests were said to have been present." [This] estimate [is] slightly in excess of the one given by the statistically minded reporter of *The New York Times* [who] placed the number present at 2,500, although he said that invitations had been sent to 3,000.
>
> This garden party deluxe was held on the grounds of Chateau-Sur-Mer, one of the most magnificent houses in Newport, on the ocean side of Bellevue Avenue. Music, the *Times* tells us, was furnished by the Germania Musical Society, whose conductor, Mr. William Schultze, produced a special "Fête Champêtre March" for the occasion. There was a pavilion for dancing, 100 feet square, and for this and other temporary pavilions, 32,000 square feet of lumber was used, as well as $2,000 worth of canvas. Wreaths and bouquets of choice flowers were flung about in the wildest profusion. Ladies wore morning costume with bonnets, and the gentlemen kept their hats in hand! Present to make the day complete for the fair sex were two young members of the British peerage, "unmarried"; the British and Russian Ministers (marital state not noted), and the visitors from the 40 yachts then lying in the Newport Harbour. Refreshments in charge of that accomplished colored chef, "Downing," who seemed to regard the whole affair as his apotheosis,

Chateau-Sur-Mer, a formidable stone "cottage" by the sea (*Culver Pictures, Inc.*)

The gloomy grandeur of Chateau-Sur-Mer's morning room (*The Preservation Society of Newport County, Newport, R.I.*)

The great staircase at Chateau-Sur-Mer (*The Preservation Society of Newport County, Newport, R.I.*)

were truly ample and varied. In fact, no abridgement of the menu could possibly do it justice, so we quote it in toto as given in the *Times*:

Card of Refreshments

Fresh Salmon à la Montpellier	Galantine of Turkey
Woodcocks	Galantine of Ham
Chicken Partridges	Galantine of Tongue
Pickled Oysters	Boned Partridges in Jelly
Crisp Potatoes à la Downing	Croquettes of Chicken
Maraschino Jelly	Chicken Salad
Rum Jelly	Lobster Salad
Wine Jelly	Italian Salad
	Celery Salad
Golden Plover	Pâté de Foie Gras
Snipes	Pâté de Truffles
Fried Oysters	Scalloped Oysters
Soft Crabs	
Ice Creams: Vanilla, Almond, Pistachio, Strawberry, Lemon	Statuettes of Lafayette and Washington
Mille Fruits Ice	Vases of Fancy Creams
Mille Fruits Crème	Nesselrode Pudding
Variety of Sherbets	Plum Pudding Glacé
Fancy Ices	Meringue Baskets à la Crème
	Jelly Russe
Fancy Cakes	Charlotte Russe
	Bonbons

Peaches, apricots, pears, nectarines, and 250 pounds of black Hamburg grapes from Mr. Wetmore's own hothouse; 24 baskets of champagne frappe, and Amontillado sherry, 6 bowls of lemonade, Sangureis, Madeira, cognac, etc.

Although you may not be planning a garden party on quite the same scale as the Wetmores, a smaller version is a lovely way to entertain on a summer's day. So here, for your daughter's wedding reception, a gala benefit, or "just because," is a modern-day menu and recipes based on some of the same dishes served on that notable day in Newport.

Galantine of Veal*
Crisp Potatoes à la Downing*
Lobster Salad*   Italian Salad*
Scalloped Oysters*
Rolled Watercress Sandwiches
Hot Rolls
Meringue Baskets à la Crème*
Champagne

ह**

GALANTINE OF VEAL

1 3-pound breast of veal
Salt
Pepper
Thyme
Marjoram
Rosemary
1 pound ground spicy sausage
½ pound ground veal
½ cup chopped walnuts
¼ cup cognac (or good Madeira)
½ pound lean ham, cut into thin strips
6 large black pitted olives, cut into large slivers
2 hard-boiled eggs
1½ quarts chicken stock
1 tablespoon gelatin
¼ cup Madeira
Watercress

Have your butcher bone the breast of veal.
Spread the breast of veal out flat and sprinkle lightly

* Recipe follows.

with salt, pepper, thyme, marjoram, and rosemary. Combine the sausage, ground veal, walnuts, and cognac. Spread over the breast of veal, leaving a 1-inch border all around. Arrange the ham strips in an even row down the length of the breast. Place rows of the olive slivers between the ham strips. Place the eggs on one side of the breast. Roll up the breast lightly and sew it well with thread and a sturdy darning needle. Wrap the roll in cheesecloth and tie the ends securely together.

Bring the stock to a full boil in a large saucepan. Gently lower the galantine into it. Reduce the heat and let simmer for 2 hours. Remove the galantine and set the stock aside. Unwrap the galantine from the cheesecloth and pat dry. Wrap in a fresh dry cloth, place on a platter, and weigh down with a flat board and a 5-pound weight (a small bread board and a heavy iron will do nicely). Refrigerate for 12 hours or longer, with the weights.

After the stock has been removed from the heat, reduce to 2½ cups and let stand for 30 minutes. Strain through a cheesecloth. Soften the gelatin in the Madeira and stir into the clarified stock. Place over a moderate heat and stir until the gelatin has dissolved. Pour into a shallow pan and refrigerate until firm and ready to use.

Unwrap the galantine and remove the thread. Chop the aspic and spread it on a chilled platter. Arrange the chilled galantine on top and garnish with watercress.

Makes 12 servings.

34

CRISP POTATOES À LA DOWNING

6 large potatoes
2 teaspoons salt
3 tablespoons butter
¼ teaspoon pepper
½ cup cream
2 egg whites
2 tablespoons grated Parmesan cheese
1 tablespoon buttered bread crumbs

Preheat oven to 375° F.

Wash, peel, and chop the potatoes. Place in a saucepan with 1 inch of boiling water and 1 teaspoon of the salt. Cover and cook until the potatoes are tender but not mushy.

Drain the potatoes, if necessary. Mash, until fluffy, with the butter, the remaining 1 teaspoon of salt, and the pepper and cream.

Beat the egg whites until stiff and fold them into the potatoes.

Grease a long, shallow baking dish generously with butter. Fill with the potato mixture. Combine the cheese and bread crumbs and sprinkle over the surface of the potatoes. Place in the preheated oven until the surface of the potatoes is lightly browned—about 15 minutes.

Serve at once.

Makes 8 to 10 servings.

ॐ

LOBSTER SALAD

4 2-pound lobsters (or larger)
2 cups chopped celery
Coral Dressing (see recipe below)
2 heads Boston lettuce
1 cup sliced boiled beets, cold
Hard-boiled eggs, sliced
Ripe olives
Pimiento strips
Watercress sprigs
Capers
Mayonnaise

Plunge the lobsters into a large kettle of boiling water. Boil for 20 minutes. Remove and cool.

Split the lobsters in half. Remove and reserve the coral for the Coral Dressing. Remove the meat and cut into small bite-sized pieces. Refrigerate until ready to serve.

Combine the lobster meat, celery, and Coral Dressing. Toss well.

Tear the lettuce into bite-sized pieces. Combine with the lobster mixture. Spoon into a large salad bowl. Decorate the surface of the salad with the beets, egg slices, olives, pimiento strips, watercress, capers, and swirls of mayonnaise.

Makes 8 to 10 servings.

Coral Dressing

Coral from 4 boiled lobsters
2 hard-boiled egg yolks
1 tablespoon mustard
¾ cup salad oil

⅓ tablespoon vinegar
½ teaspoon salt
¼ teaspoon pepper
½ teaspoon confectioners' sugar
1 egg yolk, lightly beaten

Mash the lobster coral with the hard-boiled egg yolks and mustard. With a wire whisk beat in the salad oil, vinegar, salt, pepper, and sugar. Beat in the lightly beaten egg yolk.

Makes 8 to 10 servings.

ॐ

ITALIAN SALAD

2 heads Boston lettuce
1 large bunch watercress
1 head romaine lettuce
1 slice stale French bread
1 clove garlic, peeled and split
1 tablespoon olive oil
2 tablespoons chives
1 small can anchovies in oil
8 to 10 small pitted black olives
3 tablespoons oil
1 tablespoon vinegar
1 teaspoon salt
Pepper

Separate the greens, discarding any bruised leaves and tough stems. Wash thoroughly under cold running water. Drain in a colander. Tear or break the greens into bite-

Newport on a summer's day. Even then the beaches were crowded.
(*The Rhode Island Historical Society*)

The French influence takes over in the drawing room at Chateau-
Sur-Mer. (*The Preservation Society of Newport County, Newport,
R.I.*)

sized pieces. Place on paper toweling and blot thoroughly dry. Wrap in wet paper toweling and refrigerate until well chilled.

Rub the bread with the garlic. Sprinkle with the 1 tablespoon olive oil. Break the bread into small pieces and place in a large salad bowl. Unwrap the greens and add to the bowl along with the chives, anchovies, and olives. Toss well.

Combine the 3 tablespoons oil and the vinegar and salt. Add pepper to taste. Blend well and pour over the greens. Toss and serve at once.

Makes 6 to 8 servings.

ॐ

SCALLOPED OYSTERS

48 freshly shucked small oysters and their juice
2 cups milk
2 egg yolks, lightly beaten
4 cups crumbled unsalted crackers
4 tablespoons butter, cold
Salt
Freshly ground black pepper

Preheat oven to 350° F.

Drain the oysters and set aside. Combine the oyster juice, milk, and egg yolks. Blend well.

Line a well-buttered large oblong baking dish with some of the crumbled crackers. Cover with a layer of the oysters and dot with slivers of the butter. Sprinkle lightly with salt and pepper. Repeat the layering with the cracker crumbs, oysters, butter, and salt and pepper until all the ingredients are used, ending with the crackers. Pour the oyster-juice mixture over the surface.

Place in the preheated oven. Cover and bake for 30 minutes. Uncover and continue baking until the surface is lightly browned.

Makes 8 to 12 servings.

ੜ

MERINGUE BASKETS À LA CRÈME

4 egg whites
1 cup granulated sugar
½ cup confectioners' sugar
1 pint heavy cream
½ teaspoon almond extract
1 quart vanilla ice cream
Almond slivers
8 maraschino cherry halves

Preheat oven to 200° F. to 225° F.

Grease 2 cookie sheets and coat with flour. Shake off excess flour and set aside.

Place the egg whites in a large mixing bowl and beat with an electric or rotary beater until they begin to hold a shape—about 3 minutes. Sprinkle half of the granulated sugar over the surface and continue to beat at a high speed for about 1 minute. Add the remaining granulated sugar gradually, beating while it is added. Continue to beat until shiny and stiff enough to stand in peaks.

Spoon the meringue into a pastry bag fitted with a number 7 tube and press out 8 oval shells about 1½ inches wide and 4 inches long. Sprinkle each lightly with the confectioners' sugar.

Place in the preheated oven and bake for about 2½ hours. Remove from the oven and lift the meringues with a spatula from the baking sheet to wire racks. Let stand for 2 to 3 hours before using.

Whip the cream until stiff. Fold in the almond extract.

Fill the meringue shells with the ice cream. Cover the ice cream completely with the whipped cream. Garnish with almond slivers and top each serving with a maraschino cherry half.

Serve at once.

Makes 8 servings.

Gradually sheer quantity gave way to slightly less gargantuan menus, and down-to-earth American fare was infiltrated with a touch of French *haute cuisine*. By the mid-1880's the continental motif was well established, as evidenced by the following recipes taken from the Ocean House menu used on the occasion of the Twenty-third Regiment dinner on July 5, 1886. The dishes were still lavish, but it is evident that a more sophisticated approach to food was definitely on the way.

ຂ໑

BAKED BLUEFISH À L'ITALIEN

1 4-pound bluefish
1 teaspoon garlic salt
2 teaspoons black pepper
6 tablespoons butter
1 medium onion, finely chopped
1 clove garlic, finely minced
3 cups fresh bread crumbs
1 large tomato, peeled, seeded, and chopped
½ teaspoon oregano
¼ cup dry white wine
6 thin slices salt pork

Twenty-Third Regiment.

N. G., S. N. Y.

OCEAN HOUSE,

NEWPORT.

R. I.

John G. Weaver & Son,

1886.

Menu cover from the
Ocean House,
Twenty-third
Regiment dinner
(*The Rhode Island
Historical Society*)

Menu for the Twenty-third
Regiment dinner
at Ocean House (*The
Rhode Island Historical Society*)

DINNER.

JULY 5th, 1886.

POTAGE.
Consommé de Volaille au Vermicella.

POISSON.
Baked Blue Fish à l'Italiene.
Pommes Gastronme.

RELEVES.

| Capon au Fine Herbes, | | Beef Braised à la Provencale. |

ENTREES.
Escolope of Veal Sauté à la Macedoine,

Spuguettes à la Milanaise.

ROAST.

| Beef, | | Lamb, Mint Sauce. |

COLD MEAT.

| Roast Beef, | Ham, | | Corned Beef, |
| | Lamb, | Tongue. | |

VEGETABLES.

| Boiled Potatoes, | Mashed Potatoes, | | Stewed Tomatoes, |
| String Beans, | Beets, | | Rice. |

PASTRY.
Tapioca Pudding with Apples, Hard Sauce.

| Whortleberry Pie, | | Apple Pie, |
| Assorted Cake, | | Lemon Ice Cream. |

DESSERT.

| COFFEE. | FRUIT. | CHEESE. |

Elisha Dyer accompanies Miss Laura Swan to Newport's Casino.
(*Brown Brothers*)

Slit the fish down the side and remove the backbone, or have your fish man do it for you.

Wipe the fish dry and rub inside with the garlic salt and 1 teaspoon of the pepper. Melt the butter in a large heavy skillet and sauté the onion and garlic over a low heat until golden but not brown. Add the bread crumbs, tomato, oregano, wine, and the remaining 1 teaspoon of pepper. Blend well and stuff the fish with the mixture. Place the fish in a shallow well-buttered baking dish.

Blanch the salt pork in boiling water, drain, and pat dry. Cover the top of the fish with the pork slices. Bake at 350° F. for 45 minutes, or until the fish flakes easily with a fork and the pork slices are crisp. If the fish seems too dry while baking, baste with a little white wine.

Makes 6 to 8 servings.

ಶ್

CAPON AUX FINES HERBES
(Capon with Herbs)

2 small capons
½ cup finely chopped parsley
⅓ cup finely chopped chives
4 tablespoons butter, at room temperature
2 tablespoons fine bread crumbs
2 tablespoons dry white wine
1 teaspoon salt
1 teaspoon pepper

Have the butcher split the capons and remove the backbones.

Preheat oven to 400° F.

Loosen the skin covering the breasts by slipping the fingers gently under the skin.

Combine the parsley, chives, butter, bread crumbs, and

wine and mix to form a smooth paste. Stuff each capon so that the breast meat is completely covered.

Roast uncovered in the preheated oven for about 35 minutes or until golden brown and tender. Baste frequently with the pan juices.

Makes 4 servings.

ह≈

ESCALOPE OF VEAL SAUTÉ À LA MACÉDOINE

1½ pounds leg of veal
½ teaspoon salt
½ teaspoon pepper
2 tablespoons flour
3 tablespoons butter
8 mushrooms, finely sliced
2 shallots, finely chopped
½ medium-sized green pepper, finely chopped
2 stalks celery, finely chopped
1 cup dry white wine
½ tablespoon chopped parsley

Cut the veal into ¼-inch slices. Flatten the slices with a heavy mallet, sprinkle with the salt and pepper, and dust lightly with the flour. Melt the butter in a heavy sautéing pan and brown the scallops on both sides. Transfer to a shallow baking dish and place in a low 350° F. oven while you make the sauce.

In the butter remaining in the pan sauté the mushrooms, shallots, green pepper, and celery until tender. Add more butter, if necessary. Add the wine and cook, stirring frequently, over a medium heat until the liquid is reduced by half.

Pour over the veal, sprinkle with the parsley, and serve at once.

Makes 8 servings.

ॐ

LEMON ICE CREAM

4 egg yolks
¾ cup sugar
¼ teaspoon salt
2 cups light cream
1 tablespoon grated lemon rind
½ teaspoon lemon extract
1 cup heavy cream

Beat the egg yolks slightly and combine with the sugar, salt, light cream, and grated lemon rind. Cook, stirring constantly, in the top half of a double boiler over barely simmering water until the custard thickens and coats the spoon. Add the lemon extract and blend. Pour into a large nonmetal mixing bowl and place in refrigerator to chill well.

Beat the heavy cream until stiff and fold into the custard. Cover the bowl with foil, sealing tightly, and freeze for 1½ to 2 hours or until mushy. Beat well with a rotary beater, cover again, and freeze for 3 to 4 hours.

Makes 6 to 8 servings.

NOTE: The freezing can be done in ice-cube trays, but the bowl method is simpler and easier to handle.

CHAPTER 5

Clambakes, Clams, and Food from the Sea

To the uninitiated a clambake sounds like a simple, informal beach picnic. Nothing could be further from the truth. A Rhode Island clambake in general, and a Newport bake in particular, is a time-honored, tradition-laden ritual that is never altered. And why should it be? Who would dare tamper with perfection?

Roger Ward, curator of the Newport Historical Society, outlines the procedure as follows: First, drinks are served. These are nothing as complicated as a martini, however; more likely they are Scotch or bourbon, and the more effete may be allowed a gin and tonic. This is followed by quahaugs on the half shell, well laced with horseradish, lemon juice, and pepper sauce. Then comes the chowder, at least two bowls of it. By this time the bake master is ready to "break the bake," and everyone is supposed to gather to watch this momentous event. The real business of the bake begins.

What goes into the bake and just how it is done is best

described in the Old Stone Bank's *History of Rhode Island*, in the chapter "His Honor the Clam":

Clams, bushels of them, have already been dug for the feast and deposited in some shady spot nearby. Those selected are usually about two inches long, of the white soft-shell variety found in great abundance along Rhode Island's shores. While the crowd gathers, preparations get under way for the feast. A roaring fire has been built in an open clearing, and as the flames from the crackling "four foot lengths" leap into the air, an ample supply of round field stones or cobblestones is thrown into the blaze to remain until heated to a white heat. Judging the proper heat of the stones is most important, as insufficient heating will ruin all that is to follow. When the master of the bake gives the word, great heaps of trailing marine growth called rockweed are piled on the heated stones, which have been cleared of all embers and ashes. Sometimes protected by light screening for easier handling, the clams—in the shells, of course—are heaped upon the then steaming rockweed. On top of them more weed, and on this white and sweet potatoes still in their jackets, sweet corn encased in the thin covering of their husks, large slices of mackerel, bluefish, or swordfish packaged in paper bags or cheesecloth, together with tiny sausages wrapped in the same manner. Old-fashioned dressing and peeled onions are then added to the same layer with the fish and sausages, and the great mound is then quickly covered with a heavy tarpaulin, which is well battened down with timbers and weighty stones.

Then what happens? The white-hot stones immediately transform the salt-water moisture from the rockweed, and the natural clam juice, into a fragrant, penetrating steam. The clams are baked by the moist heat from the stones, and the rising steam thoroughly cooks the rest of the pile, imparting a true tang of the sea to everything enclosed in the canvas covering.

Now to the long, rough tables, in the open generally, where strictest informality prevails regardless of the honored positions in life of distinguished guests and participants. Sometimes a coarse white cloth covers the scene of action, sometimes newspapers answer the purpose, and in most cases, the bare pine planks serve properly and satisfactorily. Coats, vests, collars, and ties are removed, and belts are unloosed. An unmistakable fragrant breeze is wafted from the steaming pile, tantalizing the eager diners while the "bake is served." Tables are already covered with dishes of sliced cucumbers, tomatoes, raw onions, radishes, and olives. Great pyramids of brown bread and white bread are within an arm's length. In fact, everything served, from start to finish of this historic "gorge," can be reached without the annoying delays of passing.

The veterans nibble excitedly at everything in sight while the neophytes, on the strength of previously absorbed advice to eat heartily, bravely pitch right in. In the midst of this preliminary attack, waiters flock from all sides with great, deep dishes of "little necks on the half shell" or small mixed quahaugs, with the meat temptingly resting in the opened shells; a dash of Tabasco sauce, a drop or two of vinegar, perhaps a dab of horseradish, and down goes the delicious morsel.

Just a word here about the clambake waiter. No royal butler serves his master more meticulously than does the bake waiter who aids and abets his or her particular responsibilities at the trencher. Regardless of capacity, long after the limit has been reached and passed, the enthusiastic waiter not only urges but begs all to eat more of everything.

Little time is allowed for the quahaug course. Back again the waiters rush with tall, two-handled tureens filled to the brims with steaming Rhode Island clam chowder. Those nearest the tureens readily do the ladling, and the bowls or soup plates provided on the tables are unusually capacious. It is a breach of etiquette not to accept at least two helpings, and three portions are the rule rather than the exception.

While the diners are engrossed in the consumption of chowder and the inevitable pilot crackers, or hard tack, the men at the bake hole or bake pile remove the huge canvas cover from the sizzling heap, and no time is lost in making the transfer to the tables. The baked or roasted clams are brought first in small two-quart pans, and other waiters follow in quick succession with the corn, potatoes, fish, sausages, and dressing.

Generally, the clams are served in double pans, one over the other to retain the heat during transportation, and to

August at the seashore as seen in *Harper's Weekly*, August 27, 1859
(*The Picture Decorator, Inc.*)

supply the diner with a spare receptacle to receive the empty shells. The heat has parted the shells of the bivalves, so no effort is required to remove the delicacy from within. At the side of each plate is a dish of melted butter and also a dish of hot clam broth. The clam is grasped at the snout with thumb and forefinger, dipped into the tangy clam water, swished through the golden yellow butter, dropped with the hand and arm, describing a majestic curve through the air, and into the watering mouth.

There is no other gastronomic evolution known to civilization that resembles in the least this peculiar and accepted arm, hand, and mouth motion so delightedly demonstrated during the baked-clam course. The process is repeated ad infinitum. Fresh and piping hot supplies are pressed upon the voracious Epicureans. Between bites ample justice is done to the auxiliary foods, no individual supply of which is allowed to suffer by the eagle-eyed waiters.

Some pile the shells on the table, others use the spare pans, while it is no uncommon sight to see a past master dexterously heave them over the left shoulder. In some sections of the state the baked-clams course remains the order of the moment until the pile of empty clam shells on the table before the diner completely obscures the neighbor across the table.

Then follow the lobsters, either boiled or broiled and served with melted butter and vinegar. Some of the more pretentious bakes include French-fried potatoes, but the ordinary occasion offers nothing more than the lobster itself, with a replenished supply of brown bread. After the lobsters the iced watermelon is brought on, followed, with time-honored adherence to a tradition, by Indian pudding and hot coffee. It seems incredible, in the face of all that has gone before, but it is common for the waiters to receive whispered inquiries from insatiable diners in regard to the possibilities of procuring just one more pan of hot ones.

You will probably have to travel to Newport, or at least to Rhode Island, to participate in a genuine clambake, and it will be well worth the trip. In the meantime, however, there are any number of delectable ways to prepare

"His Honor the Clam." Here for the sampling are some of the best, gathered from Newport's knowledgeable clammers.

ह

NEWPORT CLAM CHOWDER

1 quart freshly opened clams and their juice
¼ pound salt pork, diced
4 medium onions, peeled and chopped
4 large potatoes, peeled and diced
4 cups water
Salt
Pepper
1 quart milk
2 tablespoons butter
1 tablespoon flour
6 soda crackers, crumbled

Strain the clam juice through a fine-meshed sieve lined with a double layer of cheesecloth. Set aside.

Separate the hard part of the clams from the soft. Chop the hard portion finely. Set the soft portion aside.

Place the salt pork in a large soup kettle over a medium heat. When the pork has rendered some of its fat, add the onions and cook, stirring often, until the onions are limp. Add the chopped hard clams, potatoes, and water. Let simmer gently until the potatoes are tender. Season lightly with salt and pepper.

Scald the milk in a separate pan. Cream the butter and flour to form a paste and add to the hot milk. Add the clam juice. Cook, stirring over a low heat, until smooth. (Do not allow to boil.) Add the crackers and pour into the clam and potato mixture. Add the soft clams. Blend and correct seasoning with additional salt and pepper as needed.

Serve very hot.

Makes 8 to 10 servings.

ह

CLAM PIE

4 large potatoes, boiled, peeled, and thinly sliced
1 pint freshly opened clams, drained and minced
4 tablespoons finely minced onion
Salt
Pepper
Clam juice and sufficient milk to make 1½ cups
4 eggs, lightly beaten
Dough for crust

Preheat oven to 350° F.

Butter 4 individual ramekins and line them with some of the potato slices. Top with a layer of the clams and sprinkle with the onion. Sprinkle lightly with salt and pepper. Repeat this layering process until the ramekins are filled.

Combine the clam juice and milk with the eggs. Pour about ½ cup of this liquid over each filled ramekin. Cover each with the dough. Place in the preheated oven and bake for 30 minutes, or until the crust is lightly browned and the filling bubbly hot.

Serve hot in the ramekins.

Makes 4 pies.

WICKFORD QUAHAUG PIE

2 tablespoons butter

1 tablespoon flour

1½ cups juice from quahaugs

*2 cups minced quahaug chowder clams (or well-drained
minced canned clams)*

½ teaspoon salt

¼ teaspoon salt

Wickford Biscuits (see recipe below)

Preheat oven to 400° F.

Melt the butter in a saucepan over a moderate heat;
stir in the flour and blend well. Slowly add the quahaug
juice, stirring as it is added. Cook, stirring, until the sauce
is smooth and has begun to thicken.

Place the clams in a deep baking dish. Sprinkle with
the salt and pepper. Pour the hot sauce over them. Top
with the uncooked Wickford Biscuits, placing them close
together so that the clams and sauce are completely covered.

Bake in the preheated oven for about 15 minutes.

Serve from the dish.

Makes 4 to 6 servings.

Wickford Biscuits

¾ cup white stone-ground flour

¼ cup wheat flour

1½ teaspoons baking powder

¼ teaspoon salt

2 tablespoons shortening

⅓ to ½ cup milk

Sift the stone-ground flour, wheat flour, baking powder, and salt into a mixing bowl. Cut in the shortening with a fork until the consistency is like fine meal. Slowly add the milk; the dough should not be too sticky.

Place on a floured bread board or a pastry canvas and roll out to a ½-inch thickness. Cut with a floured biscuit cutter.

Makes 8 2-inch biscuits.

NOTE: If you do not wish to use the biscuits in the Wickford Quahaug Pie, bake on an ungreased baking sheet in a preheated 450° F. oven for about 15 minutes.

ह❧

BAKED CLAMS NORMANDE

24 large unopened clams
2 tablespoons butter
2 tablespoons finely minced shallots
4 mushrooms, finely chopped
1 tablespoon minced chives
5 tablespoons fresh bread crumbs
¼ cup dry white wine
1 tablespoon butter

Preheat oven to 350° F.

Scrub the clams well and place in a large kettle with just enough water to cover the bottom. Cover and cook over a high heat until the shells open. Remove the clams from the shells and reserve the shells. Chop the clams very fine.

Melt the 2 tablespoons butter in a small skillet and sauté the shallots and mushrooms for 3 to 4 minutes. Combine with the clams, chives, 3 tablespoons of the bread crumbs, and the wine. Blend well and fill the clam shells with the mixture.

Sprinkle with the remaining 2 tablespoons of bread crumbs, dot with the 1 tablespoon butter, and bake in the preheated oven for 15 to 20 minutes or until golden brown.

Makes 6 servings.

ဒ&

CLAMS NEWPORT CASINO

*48 unopened clams
6 tablespoons butter
2 teaspoons anchovy paste
1 tablespoon finely minced green pepper
4 pimientos, cut into 48 strips
12 uncooked bacon slices, each cut into 4 small pieces*

Open the clams and loosen them from the shells. Discard the top shells. Cream the butter and anchovy paste and place a small dab on the bottom of each shell. Place the clams over the butter.

Set the shells firmly on a bed of rock salt in a shallow baking pan and top each clam with a pinch of the pepper and a strip of the pimiento. Cover with 1 piece of the bacon.

Broil for 6 to 8 minutes. Serve at once.

Makes 8 servings.

ဒ&

CLAMS MARINIÈRE

*48 unopened clams
1 cup dry white wine
1 medium onion, peeled and quartered*

1 tablespoon minced parsley
1 bay leaf
1 tablespoon butter

Scrub the clams well, place in a large kettle, and add the remaining ingredients. Cover and cook over a high heat for 6 to 8 minutes, or until the shells open.

Pile the clams in individual soup plates and strain the cooking liquid over them. Serve at once.

Makes 8 servings.

CLAM HASH

20 large clams, shelled
3 eggs, lightly beaten
¼ cup clam juice
3 medium potatoes, boiled, peeled, and chopped
1 tablespoon minced chives
6 mushrooms, finely chopped
½ teaspoon salt
½ teaspoon pepper
3 tablespoons butter
Chopped parsley

Put the clams through the coarse blade of a food chopper and combine with the eggs, clam juice, potatoes, chives, mushrooms, salt, and pepper.

Melt the butter in an omelet pan and add the clam mixture. Cook, stirring once or twice, for 4 to 5 minutes, then allow to brown on the bottom without stirring.

Fold in half and slide onto a serving dish. Garnish with chopped parsley and serve at once.

Makes 6 servings.

CHAPTER 6

McAllister Days

66 "Never did anyone labor more devotedly for a more
trivial cause" was the rather spiteful epitaph of
one of Ward McAllister's biographers. The cause was not
entirely trivial, however, for it did enable McAllister to
make a pleasant living in what was, to him, a most agreeable
way. Like most notable careers, his began with a great idea.
In the early 1870's, "society" consisted of solidly established
old families, rich in tradition as well as hard cash, but there
was another force abroad in the land: the clever, resource-
ful, "new rich" multimillionaires anxious to spend their
wealth—and anxious, above all, to enter the sacred circle
of society.

McAllister's idea was to help them do it. Of impeccable
background himself, he found it relatively easy to set up
an ultraexclusive club, the Patriarchs, composed of five
men who, in his words, "had the right to create and rule
society." Each member was allowed to invite four ladies
and five gentlemen to the Patriarchs' balls, and it took but

A formal portrait of the formidable Ward McAllister (*Courtesy of The New-York Historical Society, New York City*)

little persuasion on McAllister's part to see that right-thinking new millionaires (those with excellent manners, of course) were included.

Grateful beneficiaries of McAllister's social approval were not lacking in expressing their appreciation in tangible ways, and his modest inherited income was generously supplemented. Stock-market tips or a discreetly paid wine merchant's or tailor's bill were accepted as a matter of course—and why not? McAllister had indeed performed a wanted service, and it was a little enough price to pay.

McAllister's plan, like all successful ones, came at the right time. The dike was cracking a bit. The distinguished Perry family had allowed their daughter to marry the rich but socially questionable August Belmont, and when the majestic Caroline Schermerhorn became Mrs. William Astor, the waves of new money overran the ramparts of the old guard. Mrs. Astor, finding herself married to one of the "new rich," condescended to become McAllister's patroness, and together they launched Newport. They were a formidable team.

Under the wing of Mrs. Astor, McAllister worked miracles of a sort. He was both an epicure and a perfectionist, a master at balancing a menu or a guest list, and it was he, under the tutelage of Mrs. Astor, who reduced society to "The 400." Without doubt, he was the father of the Newport social image. Until McAllister, Newport had been society's summer retreat—now it became a radiant summer festival.

McAllister tells us in his memoirs that simplicity was the keynote to Newport entertainment, and it does seem as though outdoor picnics and suppers were favorites. Like Marie Antoinette playing at being a milkmaid, however, they were more gala fetes than simple country amusements. Iced champagne replaced cider, menus ran to seven and eight courses, footmen and butlers served the food, and an

Mr. and Mrs. August Belmont and Mrs. Belmont's sister, Isabella
Perry (*Courtesy of The New-York Historical Society, New York
City*)

Mrs. William Astor, the first grande dame of Newport (*Courtesy of The New-York Historical Society, New York City*)

entire orchestra was engaged to play for dancing on a specially constructed dance floor.

Like many ingenious men, McAllister preferred to use his wits rather than cash. He was famous for his picnics at his Newport "farm," but he managed these affairs at minimal expense. He would ask each guest to bring "whatever your cook does best" and a bottle of champagne. Single gentlemen were asked to bring champagne and ice cream. All were asked to bring one or two servants. A dance floor was set up for twenty-five dollars, and a band engaged for another twenty-five dollars. No mention was made of the florist's expenses, but one gathers that McAllister obtained his luxurious effects by helping the florist obtain the business of McAllister's rich friends. Now, what better way to entertain two or three hundred guests for fifty dollars?

Apparently, however, his friends finally wearied of him. He was a pompous little man, totally obsessed with social position. As his beloved "400" grew more sophisticated and more traveled, they became bored by the narrow confines of McAllister's world. When he published his book, *Society As I Have Found It*, in 1890 his influence was on the wane, and the vapidity of the book finished him. Though the book was written with the best will in the world, his flowery phrases made his interesting, vital friends seem trite and dull. He was simply and solidly dropped, leaving behind a slightly ridiculous memory but a wonderful legacy of menus for dining *grand luxe*.

McAllister loved contests. He once pitted his southern cook against a friend's French chef in a soft-shell crab competition—the winner was never decided, but the crabs were superb.

BROILED SOFT-SHELL CRABS

(as prepared by Ward McAllister's southern cook)

12 soft-shell crabs
12 teaspoons butter
½ cup lemon juice
Toast points
Chopped parsley
Lemon slices

Clean the crabs per instructions on page 144. Place the crabs in a shallow baking pan, tucking the claws close to the body. Top each with 1 teaspoon of the butter. Put under a high broiler flame and heat for 8 minutes, turning once.

Preheat oven to 350° F.

Pour the lemon juice over the crabs and transfer the pan to the preheated oven for 10 minutes.

Serve on freshly made toast points. Garnish with chopped parsley and lemon slices.

Makes about 4 servings.

NOTE: No other seasoning is necessary. The salt in the crabs is sufficient. This way the delicate flavor of the crabs themselves is preserved and enjoyed most.

ह**

SAUTÉED SOFT-SHELL CRABS
(as prepared by a French chef)

12 soft-shell crabs
Flour
Salt
Pepper
½ cup butter
2 tablespoons oil
Lemon juice

Clean the crabs in the following manner: Use a pair of scissors to trim the soft shell. Cut off the head about ¼ inch behind the eyes. Squeeze gently to force out the green bubble behind the eyes. Lift and bend back the tapering points on each end of the crab's soft-shelled back and remove the spongy substance under them. Turn the crab on its back and remove the apron, the long narrow piece that starts at the lower center of the shell and ends in a point.

Wash the crabs under cold running water and pat thoroughly dry with paper toweling. Dredge lightly with flour and sprinkle with salt and pepper.

Place ¼ cup of the butter with 1 tablespoon of the oil in a large heavy skillet over a medium heat. When the butter melts and starts to bubble, add 6 of the crabs, back-side down. Cook about 5 minutes. Turn and cook 3 minutes longer.

Transfer to a heated platter and sprinkle with lemon juice. Keep warm while cooking the remaining 6 crabs by the same method.

Makes about 4 servings.

*A Newport Dinner Menu from
Ward McAllister's File*

Huîtres Gratinées à la Crème*

Potage

Consommé Printanier

Oloroso Sherry

Hors-d'oeuvres

Timbales à la Demidoff*

Poisson

Trout à la Meunière*

Relevé

Noisettes d'Agneau Cussy*

Perrier Jouet Réservé

Entrée

Suprêmes de Volaille Montpersier*

Johannishberger Blue Seal 1862

Rôt

Canvas Back Duck

Salad Breakers

Château Lafitte 1869

Entremets

Baba aux Fruits*

Dom Perignon

* Recipe follows.

A cozy chat on the beach

HUÎTRES GRATINÉES À LA CRÈME

(Creamed Oysters)

36 unopened oysters
1½ cups cream
3 tablespoons melted butter
6 tablespoons grated Parmesan cheese

Detach the oysters from the shells and discard the top shells. Remove the beards. Place 1 tablespoon of the cream in each shell, replace the oyster, and sprinkle with the butter and cheese.

Arrange in a shallow baking pan on a bed of rock salt and grill for 5 to 6 minutes under a high flame.

Serve at once.

Makes 6 servings.

ॐ

TIMBALES À LA DEMIDOFF

12 artichoke bottoms
12 Timbale Cases (see pages 149–150)
3 tablespoons butter
1 pound green peas
½ teaspoon salt
1 tablespoon cream
3 cups cooked chicken, diced
12 truffle slices
1 cup Béchamel Sauce (see page 150)

The gossip of the day was exchanged over luncheon at the Casino.

Preheat oven to 450° F.

Trim the artichoke bottoms to fit the Timbale Cases. Melt 2 tablespoons of the butter in a heavy skillet and sauté the artichokes for 5 to 6 minutes. Set aside and keep warm.

Boil the peas with the salt in enough water to cover until tender. Drain. Add the remaining 1 tablespoon butter and the cream and puree in a blender or a food mill.

Place the artichokes in the bottoms of the Timbale Cases. Cover with the pureed peas, then with a layer of the chicken. Top with a slice of truffle. Moisten with 1½ tablespoons of the Béchamel Sauce.

Bake in the preheated oven for 10 minutes or until thoroughly heated. Serve at once.

Makes 6 servings.

Timbale Cases

1½ cups sifted all-purpose flour
½ teaspoon salt
½ cup butter, cut into small slivers
3 tablespoons ice water

Have all the ingredients ice cold. Combine the flour and salt and cut in the butter with a pastry blender. Sprinkle with the ice water, quickly mix into a ball, cover, and refrigerate for at least 1 hour.

Preheat oven to 450° F.

Roll the dough out onto a floured board to a ¼-inch thickness. Cut circles to fit the bottoms of muffin tins and strips to form the sides. Line the muffin tins, pressing the edges of the dough together with your fingers to form a perfect seal. Fill the lined tins with uncooked beans or rice. This keeps the pastry from swelling as it bakes.

Bake in the preheated oven for 10 minutes, then reduce the heat to 350° F. and bake for 10 minutes longer. Discard the rice or beans and remove the cases from the tins at once. Store in a dry place while the filling is prepared.

Makes 12 cases.

Béchamel Sauce

3 tablespoons butter
3 tablespoons flour
1 cup milk
¼ cup dry white wine
¼ teaspoon salt
¼ teaspoon white pepper

Melt the butter, stir in the flour, and cook, stirring constantly, over a moderate heat until well blended—1 to 2 minutes. Add the milk very slowly, stirring constantly. Cook over a medium heat for 1 to 2 minutes.

Add the white wine and continue to cook until the sauce is smooth and thick. Season with the salt and pepper.

Makes about 1 cup.

ફ≈

TROUT À LA MEUNIÈRE

6 small trout
6 tablespoons butter
6 tablespoons cream
1 tablespoon lemon juice
1 teaspoon grated lemon rind
3 tablespoons chopped parsley

Clean the trout and wipe dry with paper toweling. Melt the butter in a heavy sauté pan and brown the trout carefully over a fairly high flame. Lower the heat and cook for 5 to 8 minutes longer, or until the fish flakes easily when tested with a fork. Remove to a heated platter and keep warm.

Add the cream, lemon juice, and lemon rind to the juices remaining in the pan. Blend well and cook only until thoroughly heated. Do not allow to boil.

Pour over the trout, sprinkle with the parsley, and serve at once.

Makes 6 servings.

ૐ

NOISETTES D'AGNEAU CUSSY
(Boned and Rolled Lamb Chops with Artichoke Hearts with Mushroom Puree)

6 3-ounce (approximate) boned and rolled lamb loin chops
3 tablespoons butter
6 white-toast rounds, only slightly larger than the rolled lamb chops
¼ cup Madeira
2 tablespoons Espagnole Sauce (see pages 153–154)
12 Artichoke Hearts with Mushroom Puree (see pages 154–155)
½ cup dry bread crumbs

Bring the meat to room temperature and sauté in 1 tablespoon of the butter for about 6 minutes to each side or until done to taste. The meat should be well browned on the outside but still slightly pink in the center. Place the meat on the toast rounds on 6 heated plates.

A morning airing

Pour the cooking liquid from the pan and discard. Add the remaining 2 tablespoons butter and the Madeira and cook until reduced by about ½. Stir in Espagnole Sauce, bring to a boil, and pour over the meat.

Garnish each plate with 2 Artichoke Hearts with Mushroom Puree. Top the artichoke hearts with bread crumbs. Serve at once.

Makes 6 servings.

Espagnole Sauce
(Brown Sauce)

4 pounds veal bones, cracked
1 large onion, coarsely chopped
1 stalk celery, coarsely chopped
3 carrots, peeled and sliced
2 bay leaves
2 cloves garlic, peeled
1 teaspoon crushed peppercorns
1 tablespoon salt
¼ cup flour
12 cups water
4 large ripe tomatoes, chopped
1 cup tomato puree

Preheat oven to 475° F.

Combine the bones, onion, celery, carrots, bay leaves, garlic, peppercorns, and salt in a large roasting pan. Place in the preheated oven and bake until the bones and vegetables are browned—about 30 minutes. Turn the bones and vegetables several times to ensure even browning. Reduce the heat, if necessary, to keep from burning but do not add water to the pan.

Remove from the oven and sprinkle the bones and

vegetables with the flour. Stir until the flour has dissolved and return to the oven for 6 to 8 minutes. Transfer the bones and vegetables to a deep soup kettle.

Add 2 cups of the water to the roasting pan and cook over a moderate heat, stirring to dissolve the brown particles that cling to the bottom and sides of the pan.

Pour the liquid from the roasting pan into the kettle with the bones and vegetables. Add the remaining 10 cups water. Stir to blend. Bring to a boil and skim the surface until clear. Add the tomatoes and tomato puree. Reduce the heat and let simmer very gently for 3½ to 4 hours. Strain into containers. Cool, then refrigerate until all the fat has risen to the surface and congealed. Remove and discard the fat.

Makes about 1½ quarts.

NOTE: The sauce may be frozen and defrosted as needed, or it may be stored in refrigerator for 1 to 2 weeks.

Artichoke Hearts with Mushroom Puree

2 9-ounce packages frozen artichoke hearts
1 shallot, peeled and minced
½ pound fresh mushrooms, trimmed and chopped
2 tablespoons butter
Bread crumbs
Salt
Pepper
Butter

Cook the artichoke hearts according to the package directions. Drain and keep warm.

Sauté the shallot and mushrooms in the 2 tablespoons butter until very soft. Place in an electric blender and blend at a high speed to form a puree. Thicken with bread crumbs. Season with salt and pepper.

Spoon the puree onto the artichoke hearts, mounding high. Serve at once or dot each with butter and reheat in a 350° F. oven.

Makes 6 servings.

ह▸

SUPRÊMES DE VOLAILLE MONTPERSIER
(Chicken Breasts Asparagus and Bercy Sauce)

6 chicken breasts
2 eggs
½ cup fine dry bread crumbs
6 tablespoons butter
12 asparagus spears, tough ends removed
½ teaspoon salt
6 truffle slices
1 cup Bercy Sauce (see page 158)

Have the chicken breasts boned, but leave the third joint of the wing intact. Wipe the breasts dry with paper toweling. Beat the eggs lightly and dip each chicken piece first in the beaten eggs and then in the bread crumbs. Press the crumbs on firmly and let the chicken pieces stand 5 to 10 minutes before cooking.

Melt the butter in a deep, heavy sautéing pan and brown the breasts on both sides over a medium heat. Lower the heat and cook an additional 5 to 10 minutes or until tender. Remove to a hot platter and keep warm.

Cover the asparagus with just enough boiling water to form steam and add the salt. Cook for 4 to 5 minutes or until just tender. Drain and arrange on the platter.

Garnish with the truffle slices and serve with the Bercy Sauce.

Makes 6 servings.

An afternoon game of polo

Bercy Sauce

½ cup finely chopped shallots
3 tablespoons butter
1 cup dry white wine
1½ cups Espagnole Sauce (see pages 153–154)
2 tablespoons chopped parsley

Sauté the shallots in the butter until limp. Add the wine and let simmer until the liquid has reduced by half.

Add the Espagnole Sauce. Blend and let simmer for 10 minutes. Strain into a second pan and reheat to steaming. Add the parsley and serve.

Makes about 2 cups.

ह्ब

BABA AUX FRUITS

½ cup milk
1 tablespoon yeast
3 eggs
⅓ cup sugar
¼ cup butter, melted and cooled
1 tablespoon dark rum
2 cups flour (approximately)
¼ cup currants
Baba Syrup (see pages 159–160)
½ cup light-colored rum
¼ cup diced mixed candied fruits

Heat the milk to steaming and then cool to lukewarm. Add the yeast and stir until dissolved.

Beat the eggs until light and frothy. Then beat in the
sugar, butter, and the 1 tablespoon dark rum. Stir in the
milk and yeast mixture. Gradually add sufficient flour to
make a medium-thick dough. Set aside and allow to rise
in a warm place until double in bulk—about 3 to 3½ hours.
Stir in the currants.

Generously butter a large ring mold or 6 individual baking cups and fill barely ½ full with the dough. Again set
aside in a warm place and allow to rise until double in
bulk—about 1 hour.

Preheat oven to 350° F.

Place the mold in the preheated oven and bake until
firm and lightly browned—about 35 minutes—or until a
cake tester comes out clean. Remove from the mold to a
cake rack and let cool. Place the cake on a plate and slowly
pour the Baba Syrup over the cake. Return the cake to the
mold and pour any Baba Syrup left on the plate over the
cake surface. Let stand several hours.

Pour the ½ cup light rum over the fruits and let stand
several hours.

Turn the cake or cakes out onto a platter or individual
dessert plates. Ladle the rum and fruits over each serving.

Makes 6 servings.

Baba Syrup

⅓ cup sugar
⅓ cup water
½ cup fresh orange juice
½ cup medium-dark rum

Combine the sugar and water in a saucepan and cook,
stirring, over a low heat until the sugar has dissolved. Bring
to a full boil over a medium heat and then remove from
the heat.

Stir in the remaining ingredients. Reheat just before pouring over the cake.

Makes about 1⅓ cups.

McAllister Describes a Summer Cotillion*

The first Cotillion Dinner ever given at Newport, I gave at my Bayside Farm. I chose a night when the moon would be at the full, and invited guests enough to make up a cotillion. We dined in the open air at 6 P.M., in the garden adjoining the farmhouse, having the gable end of the house to protect us from the southerly sea breeze. In this way we avoided flies, the pest of Newport. In the house itself we could not have kept them from the table, while in the open air even a gentle breeze, hardly perceptible, rids you of them entirely. The farmhouse kitchen was then near at hand for use. You sat on closely cut turf, and with the little garden filled with beautiful standing plants, the eastern side of the farmhouse covered with vines, laden with pumpkins, melons, and cucumbers, all giving a mixture of bright color against a green background, with the whole farm lying before you, and beyond it the bay and the distant ocean, dotted over with sailing craft, the sun, sinking behind the Narragansett hill, bathing the Newport shore in golden light, giving you, as John Van Buren then said to me, "as much of the sea as you ever get from the deck of a yacht."

Add to this, the exquisite toilets which our women wear on such occasions, a table laden with every delicacy, and all in the merriest of moods, and you have a picture of enjoyment that no shut-in ballroom could present. No "pent-up Utica" then confined our powers. Men and women enjoyed a freedom that their rural surroundings permitted, and, like the lambs gambolling in the fields next them, they frisked about, and thus did away with much of the stiff conventionality pertaining to a city entertainment.

On this little farm I had a cellar for claret and a farm-

* From *Society As I Have Found It.*

Arriving at the ball

house attic for Madeira, where the cold Rhode Island winters have done much to preserve for me wines of seventy and eighty years of age. On this occasion, I remember giving them Amory of 1811 (one of the greatest of Boston Madeiras), and I saw the men hold it up to the light to see its beautiful amber color, inhale its bouquet, and quaff it down "with tender eyes bent on them."

A marked feature of all my farm dinners was Dindonneaux à la Toulouse and à la Bordelaise (chicken turkeys). In past days, turkeys were thought to be only fine on and after Thanksgiving Day in November, but I learnt from the French the turkey poultry with *quenelle de volaille*, with either a white or dark sauce, was the way to enjoy the Rhode Island turkey. I think they were first served in this way on my farm in Newport. Now they are thus cooked and accepted by all as the summer delicacy.

After dinner we strolled off in couples to the shore (a beach three-quarters of a mile in length) or sat under the group of trees looking on the beautiful bay.

My brother, Colonel McAllister, had exercised his engineering skill in fitting up my barn with every kind and sort of light. He improvised a chandelier for the center of it, adorned the horse and cattle stalls with vines and greens, fitted them up with seats for my guests (all nicely graveled), and put a band of music in the hay-loft, with the middle part of the barn floored over for dancing. We had a scene that Teniers has so often painted. We danced away late into the night, then had a glorious moonlight to drive home by.

I must not omit to mention one feature of these parties. It was the "Yacht Club rum punch," made from old Plantation rum, placed in huge bowls, with an immense block of ice in each bowl, the melting ice being the only liquid added to the rum, except occasionally when I would pour a bottle of champagne in, which did it no injury.

Tennis anyone? A scene at the Newport Casino. (*The Preservation Society of Newport County, Newport, R.I.*)

Cotillion Supper Menu

Huîtres
Coquilles avec Riz Champagne*
Ris de Veau Suprêmes*
Jambon Glacé   Caneton Rôti Froid
Asperges à la Vinaigrette
Sorbet Pamplemousse
Gâteau Meringue*
Petits Fours   Champagne

३०

COQUILLES AVEC RIZ CHAMPAGNE
(Scallops in Champagne Rice Ring)

2 cups water
¼ teaspoon salt
1½ cups long-grained rice
1 cup champagne
¼ teaspoon white pepper
1 sprig fresh thyme
1 sprig fresh parsley
1 truffle, chopped
½ pound butter
2 pounds scallops
Salt
Cayenne pepper
Watercress sprigs

Bring the water to a full boil. Add the salt, then add the rice slowly so that the water continues to boil. Reduce the heat and let simmer until almost all the water has been

* Recipe follows.

Watching tennis at the Casino in the headgear of the day—the straw
boater (*The Preservation Society of Newport County, Newport, R.I.*)

absorbed. Add the champagne, white pepper, thyme, and parsley. Let simmer until the champagne has been absorbed but the rice is still moist. Remove the thyme and parsley. Cover the pot and let the rice stand for 15 to 20 minutes or until fluffy and dry. Stir the truffle into the rice.

Meanwhile melt the butter in a large frying pan. Add the scallops and cook them quickly, turning frequently to brown all sides, for 3 to 4 minutes.

Arrange the rice on a deep serving platter. Spoon the scallops and the cooking butter onto the center. Sprinkle with salt and cayenne pepper and garnish with watercress.

Makes 6 to 8 servings.

ह

RIS DE VEAU SUPRÊMES
(Sweetbreads Supreme)

4 pairs sweetbreads
3 cups boiling water
2 tablespoons lemon juice
2 tablespoons salt
6 shallots, peeled and minced
½ pound mushrooms, trimmed and sliced
3 tablespoons butter
3 tablespoons flour
1¼ cups chicken stock
½ cup heavy cream
½ cup dry sherry
1 pimiento, cut into thin strips
¼ cup black-olive slivers

Salt

Pepper

¼ cup fine dry bread crumbs

1 tablespoon grated Gruyère cheese

2 tablespoons melted butter

Soak the sweetbreads in ice water for 45 minutes. Drain. Place in a saucepan and pour the boiling water over them. Add the lemon juice and the 2 tablespoons salt. Let simmer for 15 minutes.

Drain the sweetbreads and place immediately in cold water. Drain once more and cut into thin slices, removing all the connective tissues, membranes, and tubes.

Preheat oven to 500° F.

Cook the shallots and mushrooms in the 3 tablespoons butter for 5 minutes, stirring almost constantly. Add the flour and stir over a low heat for 2 minutes. Slowly add the chicken stock, stirring as it is added. When the mixture is blended, continue to stir over a low heat until the sauce begins to thicken. Remove from the heat and stir in the cream and sherry. Add the sweetbreads, pimiento strips, and olive slivers. Season lightly with salt and pepper.

Spoon the mixture into a long, shallow oven-proof baking dish. Sprinkle with the bread crumbs and cheese. Moisten with the 2 tablespoons melted butter.

Place in the preheated oven until the surface is lightly browned—about 5 to 10 minutes.

Makes 6 to 8 servings.

ॐ

GÂTEAU MERINGUE
(Meringue Cake)

1 1-pound package dried apricots
3 cups water
1 cup sugar
1 quarter lemon
2 tablespoons apricot liqueur
5 egg whites
Pinch of salt
1 cup extra-fine granulated sugar
1 teaspoon vanilla
2 cups heavy cream
½ cup confectioners' sugar
2 tablespoons Grand Marnier
8 candied apricot halves

Soak the dried apricots in cold water according to the package directions. Drain. Combine with the 3 cups water, the 1 cup sugar, and the lemon. Cook over a medium heat until all the water has been absorbed and the apricots are very soft. Puree in a food mill or with a wooden spoon. Stir in the apricot liqueur and set aside.

Place the egg whites in a large bowl and let stand until they reach room temperature. Add the salt and beat with a wire whisk until very stiff and almost dry. Beat in ½ cup of the extra-fine granulated sugar, 1 tablespoon at a time, beating constantly after each addition until the sugar has dissolved. Continue beating until the meringue forms a stiff peak when the whisk is withdrawn. Add the vanilla. Sprinkle the remaining ½ cup extra-fine granulated sugar over the entire surface and fold in without beating.

Preheat oven to 250° F.

Brush 2 baking sheets with vegetable oil and dust lightly

with flour. Using an 8-inch cake pan as a guide, trace 2 circles on each sheet. Spread the circles evenly with the meringue. Bake for 1 hour or until set. Remove with a spatula to a flat surface until cool and dry.

Whip 1 cup of the cream with ¼ cup of the confectioners' sugar until stiff and combine with the apricot puree. Spread the 2 meringue layers with the mixture and put together in layer-cake fashion. Whip the remaining 1 cup cream with the remaining ¼ cup confectioners' sugar and flavor with the Grand Marnier. Ice the cake with the flavored cream and decorate with the apricot halves.

Refrigerate until ready to serve.

Makes 6 to 8 servings.

WARD MCALLISTER'S PICNICS*

Newport was now at its best. The most charming people of the country had formed a select little community there; the society was small, and all were included in the gaieties and festivities. Those were the days that made Newport what it was then and is now—the most enjoyable and luxurious little island in America.

The farmers of the island even seemed to catch the infection, and they were as much interested in the success of our picnics and country dinners as we were ourselves. They threw open their houses to us and never heeded the invasion, on a bright sunshiny day, of a party of fifty people, who took possession of their dining room, in fact of their whole house, and frolicked in it to their heart's content. To be sure, I had often to pacify a farmer when a liveried groom robbed his hen roost, but as he knew that this fashionable horde paid their way, he was easily soothed. I always then remarked that in Newport, at that time, you could have driven a four-in-hand of camels or giraffes, and the residents of the island would have smiled and found it quite the thing.

* From *Society As I Have Found It.*

New York *Herald* sketch of a McAllister country fete at which
Governor Carroll pitted his hams against Mrs. Vanderbilt's par-
tridges, and McAllister matched his pâté against Governor Wetmore's sandwiches (*Culver Pictures, Inc.*)

The charm of the place then was the simple way of entertaining; there were no large balls; all the dancing and dining was done by daylight, and in the country. I did not hesitate to ask the very crème de la crème of New York society to lunch and dine at my farm, or to a fishing party on the rocks. My little farm dinners gained such a reputation that my friends would say to me: "Now, remember, leave me out of your ceremonious dinners as you choose, but always include me in those given at your farm, or I'll never forgive you."

But to convey any idea of our country parties, one must in detail give the method of getting them up: Riding on the avenue on a lovely summer's day, I would be stopped by a beautiful woman, in gorgeous array, looking so fascinating that if she were to ask you to attempt the impossible, you would at least make the effort. She would open on me as follows: "My dear friend, we are all dying for a picnic. Can't you get one up for us?"

"Why, my dear lady," I would answer, "you have dinners every day, and charming dinners too; what more do you want?"

"Oh, they're not picnics. Anyone can give dinners," she would reply; "what we want is one of your picnics. Now, my dear friend, do get one up."

This was enough to fire me and set me going. So I reply: "I will do your bidding. Fix on the day at once, and tell me what is the best dish your cook makes."

Out comes my memorandum book, and I write: "Monday, 1 P.M., meet at Narragansett Avenue, bring *filet de boeuf pique*," and with a bow am off in my little wagon, and dash on, to waylay the next cottager, stop every carriage known to contain friends, and ask them, one and all, to join our country party, and assign to each of them the providing of a certain dish and a bottle of champagne. Meeting young men, I charge them to take a bottle of champagne, and a pound of grapes, or order from the confectioner's a quart of ice cream to be sent to me. My pony is put on its mettle; I keep going the entire day getting recruits; I engage my music and servants, and a carpenter to put down a dancing platform, and the florist to adorn it, and that evening I go over in detail the whole affair, map it out as a general would a battle, omitting nothing, not even a salt spoon; I see to

Driving on Bellevue Avenue

it that I have men on the road to direct my party to the
farm, and bid the farmer put himself and family, and the
whole farm, in holiday attire.

To return to our picnic. The anxiety as to what the
weather would be was always my first annoyance, for of
course these country parties hinge on the weather. After
making all your preparations, everything ready for the start,
then to look out of your window in the morning, as I have
often done, and see the rain coming down in torrents is far
from making you feel cheerful. But, as a rule, I have been
most fortunate in my weather. We would meet at Narragansett Avenue at 1 P.M. and all drive out together. On reaching
the picnic grounds, I had an army of skirmishers, in the way
of servants, thrown out to take from each carriage its con-
tribution to the country dinner. The band would strike up,
and off the whole party would fly in the waltz, while I was
directing the icing of the champagne and arranging the
tables; all done with marvelous celerity.

Then came my hour of triumph, when, without giving
the slightest signal (fearing someone might forestall me and
take off the prize), I would dash in among the dancers,
secure our society queen, and lead with her the way to the
banquet. Now began the fun in good earnest. The clever men
of the party would assert their claims to the best dishes,
proud of the efforts of their cook, loud in their praise of
their own game pie, which most probably was brought out by
some third party, too modest to assert and push his claim.
Beauty was there to look upon, and wit to enliven the feast.
The wittiest of men was then in his element, and I only
wish I dared quote here his brilliant sallies. The beauty of
the land was also there, and all feeling that they were on a
frolic, they threw hauteur, ceremonial, and grand company
manners aside, and, in place, assumed a spirit of simple
enjoyment. Toasts were given and drunk, then a stroll in
pairs, for a little interchange of sentiment, and then the
whole party made for the dancing platform, danced, till
sunset. As at a "Meet," the arrivals and departures were a
feature of the day. Four-in-hands, tandems, and the swellest
of Newport turn-outs rolled by you. At these entertainments
you formed lifetime intimacies with the most cultivated and
charming men and women of this country.

The old stone mill, a favorite retreat for children

Top hats and velvet capes were fashion necessities at Ward Mc-
Allister's country fetes. (*Culver Pictures, Inc.*)

Menu
McAllister's Country Fete

or

Picnique Grand Luxe

Saumon Fumé
Hors-d'oeuvres Variés
Suprêmes de Volaille Camerani*
Haricots Verts au Beurre
Filet de Boeuf Prince Albert*

Buffet Froid
Jambon   Dindonneau
Asperges   Salade Champenoise*
Salade de Fruits*
Petits Fours

Champagne

ॐ

SUPRÊMES DE VOLAILLE CAMERANI
(Chicken Breasts Camerani)

2 egg yolks
2 tablespoons cold water
8 chicken breasts
1½ cups fine dry bread crumbs
1 1-pound package flat noodles
7 tablespoons butter
1 tablespoon flour
1 cup chicken stock
½ cup Madeira
Salt
White pepper

* Recipe follows.

Preheat oven to 350° F.

Beat the egg yolks with the water. Dip the chicken breasts into the egg mixture and then into the bread crumbs. Repeat the process, pressing the crumbs onto the chicken, until smoothly coated. Place on a plate and refrigerate for at least 30 minutes.

Cook the noodles according to the package directions. Drain, mix with 1 tablespoon of the butter, and spread into a shallow, flat baking casserole. Keep warm.

Melt 4 tablespoons of the remaining butter in a heavy sautéing pan and brown the chicken breasts in it over a medium heat. Add additional butter if necessary. Arrange the chicken breasts on top of the noodles.

Melt the remaining 2 tablespoons of butter in the sautéing pan over a medium heat and stir in the flour, blending to form a smooth paste. Slowly add the chicken stock and Madeira. Cook over a medium heat until the sauce is thick and smooth. Season to taste with salt and white pepper.

Pour over the chicken breasts and noodles and bake in the preheated oven for about 10 minutes or until thoroughly heated.

Makes 8 servings.

FILET DE BOEUF PRINCE ALBERT
(Prince Albert Beef Fillet)

1 4- to 5-pound whole fillet of beef
6 thin slices pâté de foie gras
3 truffles, thinly sliced
6 thin strips pork fat
1 tablespoon butter
½ cup cognac
½ cup beef stock
¼ cup finely chopped celery
1 tablespoon finely chopped parsley
Salt
Pepper

Slit the fillet almost but not completely in half lengthwise. Arrange the pâté slices on the lower half and cover with the truffle slices. Press the fillet back into its original shape and arrange the pork-fat strips evenly on top. Tie together securely with butcher's string.

Heat the butter in a deep sautéing pan to very hot. Brown the fillet quickly on all sides. When the fillet is evenly brown, pour the cognac over the meat and ignite. When the flames subside, add the stock, celery, and parsley. Cover and cook over a moderate heat for about 45 minutes.

Remove the string and pork fat before slicing. Arrange the slices on a heated platter and keep warm. Bring the liquid in the sautéing pan to a boil and immediately remove from the heat. Season to taste with salt and pepper. Strain over the fillet slices and serve.

Makes 6 to 8 servings.

ॐ

SALADE CHAMPENOISE

2 pounds potatoes
1 pound fresh green beans
4 hard-boiled eggs, sliced
1 small tin anchovy fillets
10 pitted black olives, sliced
10 pitted green olives, sliced
1 cup champagne
¼ cup olive oil
1 tablespoon Dijon mustard
Juice from 1 lemon
Salt
Pepper

Cook the potatoes in enough boiling salted water to cover. Drain and set aside until cold. Peel and slice.

Cut the beans into 1-inch lengths. Cook covered in ⅓ cup water until just tender. Drain and rinse quickly under cold running water.

In a large salad bowl arrange alternate layers of the potatoes, beans, eggs, anchovies, and olives, ending with the potatoes. Pour the champagne over the surface and let marinate for 3 to 4 hours.

Combine the olive oil, mustard, and lemon juice. Blend and pour over the salad. Sprinkle with salt and pepper. Toss lightly with a fork and spoon. Correct seasoning with additional salt if needed.

Makes 6 to 8 servings.

SALADE DE FRUITS

6 peaches
6 apricots
1 pint raspberries
1 pint strawberries
¼ pound blanched slivered almonds
1 cup sugar
1 cup champagne

Plunge the peaches into boiling water for a half minute. Hold under cold running water. Slip off the skins. Remove the stones and cut into bite-sized pieces. Cut the apricots in half and remove the stones.

Combine the peaches, apricots, raspberries, strawberries, almonds, and sugar in a large glass bowl. Let stand in a cool place (do not refrigerate) for 1 to 2 hours. Add the champagne just before serving.

Makes 6 to 8 servings.

CHAPTER 7

Newport Cottages and Their "Haute Cuisine"

If Newport seemed elegant in the 1870's and 1880's, it soon appeared provincial and bumbling in retrospect. As the last decade of the century approached, Newport began its 35-year reign as queen of the resorts. Marble mansions replaced the rambling Victorian cottages. Elaborate balls costing hundreds of thousands of dollars took the place of Ward McAllister's country fetes. McAllister himself was replaced by a new court jester, the remarkable Harry Lehr, the so-called King of the Golden Age.

Like McAllister, Harry Lehr liked the good life but did not care to work too hard to obtain it. He came along at the right moment. Bored with the pompous mannerisms of McAllister, society in general, and Mrs. Astor in particular, Newport found the audacious and amusing young man just what it needed. Lehr took over as the social lion of the day. He was gay, witty, and fun—a welcome relief from the heavy-handed McAllister. Generously paid by a champagne importer to further his prestige, Lehr, like McAllister, was not averse to accepting such favors as paid hotel and tailor's bills—he earned them—and under his tutelage, Newport became a far gayer place. He was an expert at devising imaginative parties. He once staged a dinner exclusively for dogs, and another time he dressed a monkey in full court regalia and invited all of Newport to meet the "prince."

On one occasion Lehr, upon seeing Mrs. Astor in a dazzling white dress liberally festooned with diamonds, seized a bunch of red roses from a nearby vase and shoved them at society's queen, announcing: "Here, put these on. You look like a walking chandelier; you need color." Newport was agog for days, but the queen was charmed. She was amused, and that was enough. At this time Mrs. Astor's reign was being challenged not by one but by three women, "Newport's Great Triumvirate": Mrs. O. H. P. Belmont, Mrs. Herman Oelrichs, and Mrs. Stuyvesant Fish.

Mrs. Belmont was perhaps the most spectacular of the three. She was first married to William K. Vanderbilt, and during that period she built a veritable castle, Marble House, the most expensive resort cottage in the world. Not content with this, she added a Chinese teahouse, lacquered in red and gold by a team of Chinese artisans imported especially to do the job. However beautiful, the completed teahouse lacked facilities for making tea, this detail having been overlooked. Mrs. Vanderbilt solved the problem by having a miniature railroad constructed from the main house, and footmen in full livery rode out in the tiny cars, carrying tea trays over their heads.

Mrs. Vanderbilt then did something even more spectacular; in 1895 she divorced her husband, charging him with adultery. The divorce rocked Newport, but Mrs. Vanderbilt was undaunted. Returning the following season, she immediately issued invitations to a ball, thereby serving notice that she intended to ignore society's unspoken law against divorced women. She went on to order her

The breathtaking facade of Marble House (*The Preservation Society of Newport County, Newport, R.I.*)

They dined in splendor. Marble House, Newport. (*The Preservation Society of Newport County, Newport, R.I.*)

Mrs. O. H. P. Belmont's famous lacquered teahouse (*Brown Brothers*)

daughter, Consuelo, to marry the Duke of Marlborough, and later, at the age of forty-three, Mrs. Vanderbilt married Oliver Hazard Perry Belmont. She was indeed a force to be reckoned with.

Mrs. Oelrichs was, in her own way, also a grande dame; she ran her beautiful marble-floored Rosecliff like a drill sergeant. The house, an immense replica of the Villa Trianon, was kept in a perpetual state of polished splendor. For her spectacular White Ball, the ballroom was completely decorated in white, and six large ships, the hulls painted white, were anchored in the ocean in front of her terrace. Brilliantly lighted, they gave the illusion of a full fleet of white ships shimmering in the water.

The third member of the trio, Mrs. Fish, did more than anyone of her day to break up the stilted pattern Newport had inherited from Mrs. Astor. Irrepressible, gay, and acidly witty, she chose to be a great hostess, and she was. Bored with the era in which she lived, she made fun of it, and although her guests expected her to be sarcastically rude, they had more fun at Crossways than anywhere else. She was the first Newport hostess to rebel at the boring two- to three-hour dinners and had hers served in about an hour. On one occasion she set a record with an eight-course dinner served in thirty minutes; the footmen were so anxious to meet the deadline, the guests had to hold their plates down with one hand and eat with the other.

She had a breezy, irreverent manner. "Howdy do, howdy do," she would say, impatiently. "Make yourself at home, and God knows there's no one who wishes you were there more than I do." Upon being asked if she had seen a certain prolific Mrs. So and So's last baby, Mrs. Fish replied, "I don't expect to live that long." When a friend asked her if she knew another lady was pregnant, she said, "I do. Isn't it disgusting?" She hated people to ask about the details of her house. Once a woman asked her how large it was. "I don't know," said Mrs. Fish; "it swells at night."

.

Mrs. Herman Oelrichs (center) in tucked lace under a mountain
of roses (*Brown Brothers*)

She loved feuds and promoted them energetically. An acquaintance had a male secretary who was her inseparable companion. When someone inquired as to the lady's whereabouts, Mrs. Fish pleasantly replied that she didn't know, but that one might look under the secretary. Even formidable Mrs. Belmont was no match for Mamie Fish. At the Newport Casino Mrs. Belmont grandly accused Mrs. Fish of having said she looked like a frog. Mrs. Fish appeared very alarmed. "No, no," she declared, "not a frog—a toad, pet, a toad."

For all her cutting tongue, however, she knew how to give people a good time. The stodgy dinners and the dreary musicales were not for her; there was always a surprise. It might be a series of vaudeville acts; it might be John L. Sullivan or the entire chorus from a touring production of *The Merry Widow*. Unlike many women of her day, Mrs. Fish recognized great food and great wines. Her spectacular dinner parties are still remembered by Newporters for their perfection of food, service, and decoration. Like Mrs. Oelrichs, she was a perfectionist.

Although Newport reached the pinnacle of its glory under the reign of these three queens, it by no means faded after them. Dr. Harry Barton Jacobs, who clearly lived in the grand manner, kept a diary from 1908 to 1924 consisting of the menus and guest lists for each party given at Whiteholme, his marble cottage, modeled after a French château. Luncheon and dinner menus suitable for a king are given in the doctor's own Spencerian hand; a diagram of seating arrangements is included and such homey notes as "32 for dinner, will white oval cloth be large enough?" The guest list more often than not included Mrs. Hamilton McK. Twombley, and Mrs. Twombley herself is a Newport legend.

Mrs. Twombley was the granddaughter of Cornelius Vanderbilt, and for more than fifty years she made the Newport seasons sparkle. Her fifty-room villa, Vinland,

In command: Mrs. Stuyvesant Fish (*Brown Brothers*)

The indomitable Mrs. Hamilton McK. Twombley (*Brown Brothe*

built in the Tudor style, was invariably filled with house guests—sometimes as many as thirty at a time. Invitations were issued months in advance, and a private train brought guests from New York. Entertaining presented few problems to Mrs. Twombley: Thirty-two servants staffed the house; her French chef, Joseph Donon, had been trained by Escoffier; her chauffeurs drove fifteen automobiles, and their livery matched the special shade of maroon Mrs. Twombley used for all her motorcars.

Mrs. Twombley was a notable connoisseur of food and wines; her cellars were so lavishly stocked prior to Prohibition that a generous supply still remained upon repeal. Menus Le Pavillon would be hard put to produce today were written in French, and the food was indeed the best of French *haute cuisine*. Breakfast, almost invariably served on trays in the guests' rooms, included fresh croissants and brioches. Luncheon usually featured one of Mrs. Twombley's favorite soufflés, and dinners were the classic seven-course affairs of nineteenth-century France.

This was the fabulous era of the twenties. The war was over, the country was rich, and there seemed no reason not to live as lavishly as one could afford, and Mrs. Twombley could afford to live lavishly indeed. She was typical of the superrich of her day, the people who traveled in the grand manner aboard the great luxury liners, who made famous such hotels as the Ritz in Paris and Claridge's in London, who had their clothes made by the famous couturiers and tailors, and who above all knew and appreciated great food.

Time was running out, however, for Newport and the rest of the carefree international rich; the spectacular 1929 crash of Wall Street plunged the country into the Depression, and even though some, like Mrs. Twombley, were untouched financially, Newport was never the same again. The lavish spending ended, never to be repeated. Society itself changed; and with the coming of World War II, when

Newport converted almost overnight into one of the country's most important naval bases, a serious sense of purpose replaced the carefree attitude of the past.

Today, Newport is still a famous resort; the summers are still golden, and the blue hydrangeas flower as abundantly as ever. Most of the great mansions have been turned into museums, however, and there is far more interest in restoring the historic colonial section than in lavish parties and balls. There is nonetheless still a sense of gaiety to the Newport season; people still entertain, though now more often at small dinners and picnics, and if the opulence of the past has vanished, it has been well replaced by a younger, more interesting, way of life.

Grand living was not just confined to the land, as witness the following menu from William K. Vanderbilt's yacht, *Alva*:

Menu

Déjeuner   2 Avril

Oeufs à l'Aurore*

Langouste à la Newburg*

Tournedos à la Moelle*

Pommes de Terre   Épinard

Asperges   Sauce Hollandaise

Petit Poulet Grillé au Cresson*

Salade

Crêpes aux Confitures*

Fromage

Café de Dessert

On Board the *Alva*

* Recipe follows.

Déjeuner   Menu   2 avril

Oeufs a la Aurore.
Langouste a la Newburg
Tournedos a la Moelle
Pomme de terre   Epinard
Asperge Sce Hollandaise
Petit poulet grille au
cresson
Salade
Crepes aux confitures.
Fromage
On board the Alva.
Desert
Cafe

Luncheon menu from the Vanderbilt yacht, the *Alva* (*The Preservation Society of Newport County, Newport, R.I.*)

OEUFS À L'AURORE
(Poached Eggs with Aurore Sauce)

1 9 5

*Newport
Cottages
and Their
"Haute
Cuisine"*

8 slices firm white bread
3 tablespoons butter
Salt
2 tablespoons vinegar
8 eggs
2 cups Aurore Sauce (see page 196)
Minced parsley

Cut each slice of bread with a large biscuit cutter into rounds. Melt the butter in a large saucepan and fry the bread rounds in it until crisp. Keep warm in a low-temperature oven.

In 2 small skillets heat enough water to just cover 4 eggs. Add a sprinkling of salt to each skillet. Add 1 tablespoon of the vinegar to each. Bring the water to a full boil.

Create whirlpools by stirring vigorously with a spoon, crack open the eggs, and drop 4 eggs into each pan, 1 at a time. Lower the heat and let the eggs steep in water just below the boiling point for about 4 minutes. Remove the eggs with a slotted spoon and trim with a biscuit cutter.

Place the fried bread rounds on small plates, top with the poached eggs, and spoon the warm Aurore Sauce over each. Garnish each serving with a little minced parsley.

Makes 8 servings.

Aurore Sauce

3 tablespoons butter
2 tablespoons flour
1 cup clear chicken stock
1 cup light cream
2 tablespoons dry sherry
Salt
White pepper
¼ cup tomato puree

Melt 2 tablespoons of the butter in a heavy saucepan. Stir in the flour and cook over a very low heat, stirring, for 1 to 2 minutes. Slowly add the stock, stirring as it is added. When the mixture is smooth, add the cream and continue to stir until the sauce thickens.

Add the sherry and season lightly with salt and white pepper. Add the tomato puree and blend well. Stir in the remaining 1 tablespoon butter.

Makes about 2¼ cups.

LANGOUSTE À LA NEWBURG
(Lobster Newburg)

Meat from 6 boiled rock-lobster tails
Newburg Sauce (see page 197)
Toast points
Thin pimiento strips

Cut the lobster meat into bite-sized slices and add to the Newburg Sauce just before serving.

Serve on fish-course plates. Garnish each serving with toast points and top with pimiento strips.

Makes 8 servings.

Newburg Sauce

2 tablespoons butter
1 tablespoon flour
1½ cups heavy cream
Salt
White pepper
2 egg yolks, well beaten
2 tablespoons good dry sherry

Melt the butter in a heavy saucepan over a low heat. Stir in the flour and blend well. Gradually add the cream, stirring constantly until it is thick and smooth. Do not allow to boil. Add salt and white pepper to taste.

Pour the mixture slowly over the egg yolks in the top of a double boiler, stirring constantly. Place over simmering water and cook, stirring, for about 3 minutes. Add the sherry and blend.

Makes about 2 cups.

ક્ષ

TOURNEDOS À LA MOELLE
(Tournedos with Marrow Sauce)

8 small tournedos (center slices of beef fillet)
3 tablespoons butter
2 tablespoons oil
8 toast rounds, about the same size as the tournedos
Moelle Sauce (see page 199)
Watercress sprigs

Sauté the tournedos in the butter and oil over a fairly high heat until done to taste.

Under the stately elms of Newport (*Brown Brothers*)

Place the toast rounds on serving plates. Top with the tournedos and ladle the Moelle Sauce over each. Garnish each serving with watercress sprigs.

Makes 8 servings.

Moelle Sauce
(Marrow Sauce)

Beef marrow from a large marrow bone
1 cup dry white wine
1 tablespoon chopped shallots
1 sprig thyme
½ bay leaf
⅛ teaspoon salt
2 tablespoons butter
1 tablespoon flour
1 cup concentrated beef stock or broth
2 tablespoons chopped parsley

Have your butcher extract the marrow from the bone and dice it.

Place the marrow in simmering water until soft. Remove with a slotted spoon. Drain and set aside.

Place the wine, shallots, thyme, bay leaf, and salt in a saucepan over a low heat. Let come to a boil, then lower the heat and simmer until reduced to about ⅓ cup. Strain through a colander lined with cheesecloth.

Melt the butter in a second saucepan and stir in the flour. Cook, stirring constantly, until the mixture takes on color. Slowly add the beef stock or broth, stirring as it is added. Continue to stir until thick and smooth. Add the strained wine and stir to blend.

Just before serving, add the marrow and parsley.

Makes about 1⅓ cups.

ॐ

PETIT POULET GRILLÉ AU CRESSON
(Broiled Spring Chicken with Watercress)

4 very small broilers
¼ pound butter
Salt
Pepper
½ cup chopped watercress

Have the butcher clean and split each bird in half. Have the spinal column removed from each bird.

Preheat broiler.

Melt the butter in a small saucepan. Brush the birds on both sides with the butter. Sprinkle lightly with salt and pepper and place skin-side up on a broiler rack. Broil about 3 inches from the heat for about 15 to 18 minutes, depending on size, brushing frequently with the melted butter.

Turn the halves skin-side down, brush again with the melted butter, and broil, basting frequently with the melted butter, for an additional 10 to 15 minutes, or until they are tender and golden brown. Arrange the pieces on warm serving plates.

Add the chopped watercress to the remaining butter. Place over a moderate heat until the butter is thoroughly reheated—only a few moments. Pour a little butter and watercress over each half broiler and serve at once.

Makes 8 servings.

2 0 1

*Newport
Cottages
and Their
"Haute
Cuisine"*

CRÊPES AUX CONFITURES

(Dessert Pancakes with Jam)

*1 cup milk
½ cup water
3 eggs
1 tablespoon sugar
7 tablespoons cognac
1½ cups sifted all-purpose flour
7 tablespoons melted butter (approximately)
8 teaspoons strawberry jam
8 teaspoons orange marmalade
Confectioners' sugar*

Place the milk, water, eggs, the 1 tablespoon sugar, 5 tablespoons of the cognac, and the flour in an electric blender. Blend at high speed. Use a rubber scraper to dislodge any flour that may stick to the sides of the container. Add 5 tablespoons of the butter and blend for 30 seconds. Cover and refrigerate for 2 to 3 hours.

Heat a heavy 6-inch crepe pan and brush lightly with a little of the remaining 2 tablespoons butter. When the butter begins to smoke, pour in about ⅓ cup of the batter and immediately tilt the pan in all directions to spread a thin film of batter over the entire surface of the pan. Cook for about 1 minute, sliding the pan back and forth to loosen the crepe. When the underside is lightly browned, turn the crepe and brown the second side.

Remove the crepe and spear a little of the remaining butter on the side that was cooked last. Roll. Keep warm in a low (200° F.) oven. Cook second crepe and repeat until 16 crepes have been made.

Stir 1 tablespoon of the remaining cognac into the jam

A stroll on the lawn after tea called for pristine elegance of dress and a hat of imposing proportions. Mrs. Joseph Willard with her husband. (*Brown Brothers*)

Two "Fair Ladies" marvelously erect under their staggering hats (*Brown Brothers*)

Discussing the events of the day on a morning stroll down Bellevue Avenue (*Brown Brothers*)

Mrs. Stuyvesant Fish (right) with Miss Lola Robinson (*Brown Brothers*)

and 1 tablespoon into the marmalade. Unroll and spread 8 crepes with the jam and 8 crepes with the marmalade.

Place 2 rolled crepes on each of 8 warm dessert plates. Sprinkle with confectioners' sugar and serve.

Makes 8 servings.

No little of Mrs. Hamilton Twombley's fame as a hostess was due to her chef, Joseph Donon. Though his repertoire was endless, the following recipes were among Mrs. Twombley's favorites.

ह

HOMARD À L'AMÉRICAINE
(American-Style Lobster)

6 1¼-pound lobsters
Salt
Black pepper
3 tablespoons olive oil, hot
4 shallots, finely chopped
3 cloves garlic, finely chopped
1 cup cognac
1½ cups dry white wine
*8 tomatoes, seeded and chopped (or 4 tablespoons tomato
    puree)*
1 tablespoon mixed chopped parsley and tarragon
Butter
Cayenne pepper

Insert a sharp knife between the body and the tail shells to cut the spinal cord and kill the lobsters. Then sever the claws, cut the tails into sections, split the bodies in half

Fine trappings for a Newport outing (*The Carriage Collection of
Colonel Paul H. Downing*)

lengthwise, and remove and discard the little bag near the head. Reserve the tomalley (green liver) and the coral for the sauce. Season the lobster with salt and black pepper and toss the pieces in the olive oil.

Sprinkle the lobster with the shallots and garlic and simmer for a few minutes, covered. Add ½ cup of the cognac, cover the pan, and simmer for 5 minutes. Add the wine, tomatoes, and parsley and tarragon. Cover the pan and set it in a moderate oven for 20 minutes.

Transfer the lobster to a heat-proof platter. Reduce the sauce in the pan to ⅓ its original volume and add the reserved tomalley and coral and a little butter. Cook for 1 to 2 minutes, swirl in 1 tablespoon of butter, and adjust the seasoning with salt, black pepper, and cayenne pepper.

Pour the sauce over the lobster. Heat the remaining ½ cup cognac and sprinkle over the lobster. Set ablaze and serve flaming.

Makes 10 servings.

ॐ

HOMARD LAFAYETTE
(Lafayette Lobster)

3 tablespoons butter
3 onions, peeled and chopped
12 ripe tomatoes, peeled, seeded, and chopped
6 1-pound lobsters
½ cup olive oil
6 shallots, chopped
3 cloves garlic, chopped
½ cup cognac
2 cups dry white wine
3 sprigs parsley

1 bay leaf
2 cups Rice Pilaf (see page 208)
1 cup Velouté Sauce (see page 209)
1 teaspoon chopped tarragon
6 truffle slices
Butter

Melt the 3 tablespoons butter and cook the onions in it until they are soft but not brown. Add the tomatoes and cook slowly in a covered pan for 2 hours.

First kill the lobsters by inserting a sharp knife between the body and the tail shells; this cuts the spinal cord. Sever the tails and claws from the bodies of the lobsters. Split the bodies in half and remove the stomachs and intestinal veins. Boil the bodies in salted water for 10 minutes and clean them well under running water. Set aside.

Heat the oil in a sautéing pan and cook the lobster tails and claws over a high heat, stirring constantly, until they turn red. Pour off the cooking oil. Sprinkle the lobster with the shallots and garlic and cook, covered, for 5 to 10 minutes. Add ¼ cup of the cognac, set it ablaze, and put out the fire by covering the pan. Add the wine, simmer for a few minutes, and add the tomato and onion mixture, parsley, and bay leaf. Cover the pan again and cook slowly for 20 to 25 minutes.

Remove the tails and claws from the pan. Turn the remaining contents of the pan into a colander and strain the liquid into a bowl. When the tails and claws are cool enough to handle, remove the meat whole by cutting the shells with a pair of scissors. Put the lobster meat in the sautéing pan and sprinkle it with 2 tablespoons of the strained cooking liquid. Cover the pan and set it in a warm place.

Force the nonliquid contents remaining in the colander

through a sieve and combine this with the cooking liquid. Reduce the mixture over a high heat to about 1½ cups.

Arrange the Rice Pilaf along the sides of a long platter. Warm the lobster bodies in hot water and arrange them on the platter across the rice. Put the meat of 1 tail and 2 claws on each body.

Combine the 1½ cups lobster sauce with the Velouté Sauce, add the tarragon and the remaining ¼ cup cognac, and pour a little sauce over each body. Garnish with a slice of truffle warmed in butter. Serve very hot.

Makes 6 servings.

Rice Pilaf

1 medium onion, peeled and chopped
2 tablespoons butter
2 cups uncooked rice
2½ cups boiling chicken stock
2 cups boiling water
Salt
Pepper

Preheat oven to 375° F.

Sauté the onion in the butter in a heavy casserole until soft but not brown. Add the rice and continue to cook over a low heat, stirring occasionally, until the rice turns translucent. Do not allow to brown. Add the stock and water and season to taste with salt and pepper.

Cover the casserole, place in the preheated oven, and bake for 5 minutes. Reduce the heat to 350° F. and bake until the rice has absorbed all the liquid—about 25 to 30 minutes.

Makes 8 servings.

Velouté Sauce

209

Newport
Cottages
and Their
"Haute
Cuisine"

⅓ cup butter
⅓ cup flour
3 cups chicken stock
¼ teaspoon salt
¼ teaspoon white pepper

Melt the butter in a heavy saucepan, stir in the flour, and blend over a low heat until smooth. Slowly add the chicken stock, stirring constantly to avoid lumping.

Continue to cook over a low heat until the sauce is thick and creamy—about 10 to 15 minutes.

Makes 2½ cups.

ह≈

MARYLAND DEEP-FRIED SOFT-SHELL CRABS

12 soft-shell crabs
2 eggs
½ cup milk
¼ teaspoon salt
¾ cup flour (or more as needed)
1 teaspoon baking powder

Clean the crabs (see page 210). Wash under cold water and pat thoroughly dry with paper toweling.

Beat the eggs with the milk and salt. Mix the flour with the baking powder. Dip the crabs first in the egg mixture, then in the flour.

Pour frying oil into a deep, heavy skillet to a depth of

2 inches. Heat to smoking (360° F.) and fry the crabs, 3 at a time, until golden brown—about 3 minutes.

Serve at once.

Makes about 4 servings.

CRABES MOUS MEUNIÈRE
(Soft-Shell Crabs Meunière)

6 soft-shell crabs
Salt
Pepper
1 tablespoon heavy cream
½ cup flour
½ cup clarified butter, hot
6 bread slices
1 tablespoon butter
¼ cup butter
Juice of 1 lemon
1 tablespoon chopped parsley

With a pair of scissors, cut off the segment that folds under the rear of each crab's body. Turn the crab and cut off the "face" behind the eyes. Remove the back shell. Wash the crabs well in cold running water, drain, and arrange on a shallow pan. Season with salt and pepper and sprinkle with the cream. Put the crabs in the refrigerator until just before serving time.

Dip the crabs in the flour and brown them quickly in the ½ cup clarified butter, shaking the pan constantly to keep the crabs from sticking. Turn and brown the other side. Drain.

Brown the bread slices in the 1 tablespoon butter. Serve

each crab on a bread slice. Heat the ¼ cup butter to a golden-brown color. Sprinkle the crabs with the lemon juice, parsley, and heated butter.

Makes about 3 servings.

2 I I

Newport
Cottages
and Their
"Haute
Cuisine"

ह≈

SOFT CLAMS IN CREAM SAUCE

48 unopened clams
2 egg yolks
½ cup cream
1 teaspoon chopped parsley

Open the clams and separate the soft portions from the hard. (The hard portions may be used for chowder.) Put the soft clam meat and the clam juice in a saucepan, bring the liquid to a boil, and cook for 1 minute.

Lift the clams out of the juice with a sieve. Strain the liquid through several thicknesses of cheesecloth and reduce it over a moderate heat to ⅓ its original volume. Return the clams to the reduced juice and heat.

Mix the egg yolks with the cream and blend in with the clams. Heat without allowing the sauce to boil. Add the parsley.

Makes 8 servings.

NOTE: Neither salt nor pepper is required to season this dish; the fresh clam juice is naturally salty.

ॐ

SUPRÊMES DE VOLAILLE VIRGINIENNE
(Chicken Breasts with Virginia Ham)

6 chicken breasts
2 tablespoons heavy cream
2 tablespoons flour
6 tablespoons butter, melted
6 slices white bread
6 slices cooked Virginia ham
¾ cup Madeira
1 pound mushroom caps
3 tablespoons butter
1 tablespoon lemon juice (approximately)
Salt
Pepper
1 tablespoon chopped parsley
6 truffle slices
*½ cup Espagnole Sauce (see pages 153–154) (or brown
   stock)*

Have your butcher bone and flatten the chicken breasts.

Moisten the breasts with the cream and refrigerate for
1 to 2 hours. About 30 minutes before serving, dust the
breasts with the flour and sauté in the 6 tablespoons butter
until lightly browned on both sides—about 15 minutes.
Remove to a heated platter and keep warm.

Trim the bread slices to fit the chicken breasts and
brown them in the same butter that was used to sauté the
chicken breasts. Trim the ham slices also to fit the chicken
breasts and warm the ham in ¼ cup of the Madeira. Cook
the mushroom caps for 5 minutes in the 3 tablespoons
butter with the lemon juice. Season the mushrooms with
salt and pepper and sprinkle with the parsley.

Pile the mushrooms in the center of a round serving dish. Arrange the bread slices around the edge of the dish. Top each bread slice with a slice of ham, a cooked chicken breast, and a slice of truffle.

Deglaze the pan in which the chicken was cooked with the remaining ½ cup Madeira and the Espagnole Sauce by pouring in the liquid and stirring quickly over a high heat to take up the browned particles. Reduce the liquid quickly by boiling over a high heat to half its original volume. Pour over the chicken breasts.

Serve at once.

Makes 6 servings.

ड़

PINTADES AUX GENIÈVRES
(Guinea Hens with Juniper Berries)

3 2-pound guinea hens
Clarified butter
3 tablespoons crushed juniper berries
3 tablespoons brandy
½ cup chicken stock
Salt
Pepper

Truss the wings and legs of the hens close to the bodies. Brush generously with clarified butter and roast in a hot oven (400° F.) for 15 minutes, basting frequently with additional clarified butter and the drippings. Add the juniper berries to the pan and roast for 10 minutes more, basting frequently and adding more clarified butter as needed.

Remove the hens to a heated dish. Skim off the fat from the roasting pan, return the hens to the pan, and pour the brandy over them. Stir, scraping the pan, for 1 to 2 minutes, and add the stock. Cook, stirring, for a few minutes to blend well.

Remove the guinea hens to a serving platter and cut them in half lengthwise. Correct the seasoning of the sauce with salt and pepper and strain it over the birds.

Makes 6 servings.

ह♥

CAILLES RÔTIES
(Roast Quail)

4 quail
Melted butter
Salt
Pepper
Croutons
8 tablespoons brown stock

Brush the birds well with melted butter, season with salt and pepper, and roast in a moderately hot oven (400° F.) for about 20 minutes. Baste with the pan drippings 3 times during the cooking. Brown the croutons in butter. Place the quail on the croutons.

Pour off the cooking fat and add the stock to the pan. Cook, stirring in the brown bits, for a few minutes and pour the sauce over the birds.

Makes 4 servings.

The classic French entrance to The Elms (*The Preservation Society of Newport County, Newport, R.I.*)

Framed by Newport's famous trees, the formal French garden of The Elms (*The Preservation Society of Newport County, Newport, R.I.*)

ॐ

OEUFS À LA BENEDICT
(Eggs Benedict)

6 English muffins
Butter
12 slices cooked ham
12 poached eggs
2 cups Hollandaise Sauce (see recipe below)
12 truffle slices
Meat extract

Split, toast, and butter the muffins. Put a slice of ham, cut to fit, and a poached egg on each half. The ham may be warmed in a little hot butter, if desired. Top the eggs with the Hollandaise Sauce and garnish with the truffle slices, dipped in meat extract.

Makes 6 servings.

Hollandaise Sauce

5 egg yolks
3 tablespoons hot water
3 tablespoons lemon juice
½ cup butter
Salt
White pepper

In a large mixing bowl beat the egg yolks with a wire whisk until they are thick and pale in color. Add the water and lemon juice and beat vigorously.

Heat the butter until it is just bubbly and pour it slowly into the egg mixture, beating as it is added.

Pour the mixture into a saucepan. Cook over a very low heat, stirring constantly, until the sauce thickens— about 10 minutes. Season to taste with salt and white pepper.

Makes about 1 cup.

NOTE: If the sauce begins to curdle, remove from the heat and beat in 2 tablespoons light cream. The sauce may be kept warm over hot (but not boiling) water for 15 to 20 minutes before serving.

ತನ

SOUFFLÉ AU CHOCOLAT
(Chocolate Soufflé)

¼ pound sweet chocolate
1 cup milk
2½ tablespoons sugar
3 tablespoons flour
3 egg yolks
½ teaspoon vanilla extract
1 teaspoon butter
3 egg whites
Sugar

Heat the chocolate and milk together, stirring, until the chocolate melts. Remove the pan from the heat.

Mix the sugar and flour in a bowl, add the egg yolks, and beat with a wire whisk until the mixture is very creamy. Slowly stir in the chocolate and milk.

Return this mixture to the saucepan and cook, stirring, until the sauce is smooth and thick. Add the vanilla and butter. Beat the egg whites until stiff and fold in.

Turn the mixture into a 1-quart soufflé dish, buttered and sprinkled with sugar. Bake in a moderate oven (350° F.)

for 20 to 30 minutes until the soufflé is well puffed and browned. Serve at once.

Makes 2 to 3 servings.

ello

SOUFFLÉ AU KIRSCH
(Kirsch Soufflé)

½ *cup confectioners' sugar*
½ *cup flour*
1 whole egg
3 egg yolks
2 cups milk
1 tablespoon butter
3 tablespoons kirsch
3 egg whites

Mix the sugar, flour, whole egg, and egg yolks. Scald the milk and stir it in gradually. Bring the mixture to a boil, stirring constantly, and cook for 2 minutes.

Remove the pan from the heat and stir in the butter. Cool the batter and add the kirsch. Fold in the egg whites, beaten stiff. Bake in a buttered soufflé dish in a moderate oven (350° F.) for about 40 minutes until the soufflé is well puffed and browned.

Makes 6 servings.

The following menus are from Dr. Harry Jacobs's Whiteholme files.

221

Newport
Cottages
and Their
"Haute
Cuisine"

Menu

Melons
Crabs in a Chafing Dish*
Poulet à la Maryland*
Haricots de Lima
Maïs au Beurre
Côtelettes de Pigeons Perigord
Salade de Raisins
Turban de Pêches*
Gâteaux

ॐ

CRABS IN A CHAFING DISH

10 soft-shell crabs
Salt
Pepper
Flour
¾ cup butter
Juice from 1 lemon
3 tablespoons minced parsley

Clean the crabs in the following manner: Wash under cold running water. Using a pair of scissors, cut off the heads about ¼ inch behind the eyes and discard the green bubble. Lift the soft shell where it comes to a point at

* Recipe follows.

each side and cut off the white gills. Peel back, cut off, and discard the apron. Dip each crab in salted water and then blot dry with paper toweling.

Sprinkle the crabs with salt and pepper. Dredge with flour and then shake off excess flour.

Melt the butter in a chafing dish and heat to sizzling. Add the crabs back-side down and sauté for 5 minutes. Turn and sauté for 3 to 4 minutes. Transfer the crabs to heated serving plates.

Add the lemon juice and parsley to the chafing dish. Cook, stirring, for a few seconds, then pour over the crabs and serve at once.

Makes about 8 servings.

ह⊷

POULET À LA MARYLAND
(Chicken, Maryland Style)

4 chicken breasts
3 eggs
1 teaspoon water
2 cups very fine dry bread crumbs
½ pound butter
4 bananas
8 thick slices grilled bacon
Crisp watercress
Crisp corn-bread sticks

Have the butcher bone the chicken breasts, split them in half, and remove the first 2 wing bones, leaving the main wing bone.

Put each breast between 2 sheets of waxed paper and pound thin with the flat side of a cleaver.

Lightly beat the eggs with the water. Dip each halved breast in the eggs and then roll in the bread crumbs. Place on a rack and let stand for 10 to 15 minutes.

Preheat oven to 325° F.

Melt the butter in a saucepan over a low heat. Remove from the heat and let stand for a few seconds. Slowly and carefully pour equal amounts of the butter into 2 large skillets, leaving all the white sediment in the bottom of the saucepan.

Heat the butter and carefully sauté 4 halved chicken breasts in each skillet over a low heat until the breasts are lightly browned on each side.

Transfer the chicken breasts to a long, shallow baking dish. Place in the preheated oven and bake for 20 minutes, basting frequently with the butter from the skillets.

Peel and cut the bananas in half 5 minutes before the chicken is ready to serve. Reheat the remaining skillet butter and fry the bananas in it until lightly flecked with brown.

Arrange the chicken breasts and fried bananas on 8 heated dishes. Top each halved breast with a slice of bacon and pour a little skillet butter over them. Garnish each plate with watercress and serve with corn-bread sticks.

Makes 8 servings.

NOTE: The original recipe calls for 1- to 1½-pound whole broilers split and partially boned. As such small broilers are rarely available in the general market, and few butchers are skilled at boning them, chicken breasts are the logical substitution.

TURBAN DE PÊCHES

1 cup chopped fresh peaches
2 tablespoons Grand Marnier
¾ cup sugar
1 tablespoon gelatin
⅓ cup cold water
1½ cups heavy cream
2 egg whites
Fresh peach slices

Combine the 1 cup peaches and the Grand Marnier and sugar in a large mixing bowl. Let stand at room temperature until the sugar has dissolved.

Soften the gelatin in the cold water in the top of a double boiler. Stir over hot water until dissolved. Add to the chopped peaches and stir until blended.

Pour the cream into a large mixing bowl. Place the bowl in the freezing compartment of refrigerator until icy cold. Whip with a wire whisk until very stiff.

Beat the egg whites in a second bowl until stiff. Fold first the beaten egg whites and then the peach mixture into the whipped cream.

Pour the mixture into a chilled, oiled, turban-shaped mold and chill for several hours. Unmold onto a chilled platter and garnish with fresh peach slices.

Serve at once.

Makes 8 servings.

Melons
Consommé de Tomate
Tartelettes de Crabes*
Côtelettes de Veau Maryland
Maïs à la Crème
Haricots de Lima
Mousse de Fromage*
Salade
Turban de Pêches†
Gâteaux

ह≈

TARTELETTES DE CRABES
(Individual Crab Tarts)

Tart Pastry for 8 individual tarts (see page 228)
1 egg white, lightly beaten
1 whole egg, lightly beaten
1 egg yolk, lightly beaten
1 cup light cream
2 tablespoons grated Parmesan cheese
¼ cup grated Swiss cheese
1½ cups flaked cooked crab meat
½ teaspoon salt
¼ teaspoon white pepper

Preheat oven to 400° F.

Line 8 individual tart pans with the Tart Pastry and brush with the 1 egg white. Place in the preheated oven and bake for 5 minutes, or until the pastry is just set.

* Recipe follows.
† See page 224.

The Venetian dining room of The Elms (*The Preservation Society of Newport County, Newport, R.I.*)

Combine the remaining ingredients. Blend well and spoon into the tart shells, filling them nearly to the top.

Return the tarts to the oven and bake at 325° F. until the custard has set.

Serve hot.

Makes 8 servings.

Tart Pastry

2 cups unsifted all-purpose flour
1 teaspoon salt
½ cup butter
¼ cup lard
¼ cup ice water

Sift the flour and salt into a mixing bowl. Cut in the butter and lard with a pastry blender until the mixture resembles cornmeal. Sprinkle in the water a little at a time and mix lightly with a fork until the flour is moistened.

Gather the dough into a ball, cover, and refrigerate for 15 to 30 minutes. Roll out to about ⅛-inch thickness and cut out rounds 1 inch larger than tart pans. Fit into tart tins and flute the edges with a fork.

Makes 8 tarts.

MOUSSE DE FROMAGE
(Cheese Mousse)

6 egg yolks
½ cup light cream
½ pound sharp cheddar cheese, soft

2 tablespoons gelatin
½ cup cold water
1½ cups heavy cream, well chilled
3 egg whites
Chopped watercress
Toast points

229

*Newport
Cottages
and Their
"Haute
Cuisine"*

Beat the egg yolks with the light cream in the top of a double boiler. Place over hot water and add the cheese. Stir until the cheese has melted.

Soften the gelatin in the water and add to the hot cheese mixture. Stir until the gelatin has dissolved. Remove from the heat and let stand until cool.

Beat the heavy cream until stiff. In a second bowl beat the egg whites until stiff. Fold the beaten cream and then the egg whites into the cheese mixture.

Pour the mixture into 1 large or 8 individual oiled molds. Refrigerate 3 hours or longer.

Unmold and garnish with chopped watercress. Serve with toast points.

Makes 8 servings.

NOTE: This may be served as a separate course for a formal meal or as an hors d'oeuvre.

Menu

Consommé
‾Homard à la Newburg
Filet Mignon de Boeuf avec Sauce Béarnaise*
Pommes de Terre Frites
Légumes
Chaud-froid de Poulet
Salade
Bombe de Framboise*

* Recipe follows.

Parquet, crystal, gilt, and marble: the ballroom of The Elms (*The Preservation Society of Newport County, Newport, R.I.*)

ह‍‌‍

FILET MIGNON DE BOEUF AVEC SAUCE BÉARNAISE

6 filets mignons
Butter, at room temperature
Béarnaise Sauce (see recipe below)
Watercress

Have the butcher cut the filets mignons 1½ inches thick.

Bring the meat to room temperature. Spread each fillet with soft butter. Broil the fillets about 2 inches from the flame for 5 minutes at a high heat. Turn, spread with soft butter, and broil for 3 to 5 minutes, depending on the degree of rareness desired.

Serve with a little hot Béarnaise Sauce over each steak. Garnish with watercress. Pass additional sauce at the table.

Makes 6 servings.

Béarnaise Sauce

3 shallots, peeled and chopped
2 sprigs fresh tarragon
2 sprigs fresh chervil
¼ cup fresh lemon juice
¼ cup dry white wine
2 egg yolks
2 tablespoons water
¼ pound butter, at room temperature
Salt
Pepper

233

*Newport
Cottages
and Their
"Haute
Cuisine"*

Place the shallots, tarragon, and chervil in a saucepan. Add the lemon juice and wine. Let simmer over a moderate heat until reduced to ¼ of its original volume. Remove from the heat and strain through a fine sieve. Discard solids.

Beat the yolks and water in the top of a double boiler over simmering water. Beat in the warm strained lemon juice and wine. Start adding the butter, 1 tablespoon at a time, beating after each addition until the butter has melted. Continue until all the butter has been added. Season with salt and pepper to taste.

Makes sufficient sauce for 8 steaks.

BOMBE DE FRAMBOISE
(Raspberry Bombe)

1 quart vanilla ice cream, preferably hand-packed
1 quart fresh raspberries
¾ cup sugar
2 tablespoons Grand Marnier
2 tablespoons gelatin
½ cup cold water
2 cups heavy cream
Whole raspberries

Line a greased 2-quart bombe mold with the ice cream, about ½-inch thick, pressing the ice cream against the mold with the back of a wooden spoon. Cover and place in the freezing compartment of refrigerator.

Force the raspberries through a sieve or puree in a blender. Place in a mixing bowl. Add the sugar and Grand Marnier and let stand at room temperature for 2 to 3 hours.

Soften the gelatin in the water, place over hot water in

a double boiler, and stir until dissolved. Add this to the raspberry mixture. Blend and place in refrigerator until the mixture begins to thicken.

Whip the cream until stiff. Fold the cream into the raspberry mixture. Blend and spoon into the center of the bombe mold. Cover the mold and refrigerate for 3 hours or longer.

Unmold onto a chilled plate. Garnish with whole raspberries and serve at once.

Makes 8 to 10 servings.

Menu

Melons

Consommé Montmartre

Cornets aux Champignons

Chicken Halibut Cardinal

Selle d'Agneau Rôti   Sauce Cumberland

Croquettes aux Pommes

Pois au Beurre

Poulard aux Perles de Perigord*

Salade d'Ananas

Bombe Aboukir

Gâteaux

* Recipe follows.

235

*Newport
Cottages
and Their
"Haute
Cuisine"*

POULARD AUX PERLES DE PERIGORD

(Roasted Chicken with Truffles)

*1 2-ounce can black truffles
½ cup Marsala
1 3½- to 4-pound roasting chicken
4 tablespoons soft butter
Salt*

Drain the truffles, reserving the juice. With a small, sharp knife, slice each truffle into thin rounds. Place in a shallow glass or a nonmetal dish. Add the truffle juice and the Marsala. Let marinate for 1 to 2 hours.

Wash the chicken under cold running water inside and out. Pat dry with paper toweling.

Starting at the breast, gently separate the skin from the meat by forcing your fingers between them. Slide your hand under as far as you can go and slowly free the skin on both sides of the breast. Carefully insert a rubber spatula at the breast opening, and holding the spatula flat against the flesh, move it sideways and loosen the skin around the upper part of each leg, pushing the leg in on itself to give you more traction. Stop about halfway down the leg.

Remove the truffle rounds from the marinade (reserve the marinade) and without drying them, insert them 1 at a time under the skin. Arrange them as symmetrically as possible, first on the legs and then on both sides of the breastbone. Pat and reshape the loosened skin back into place. It will sag slightly but will pull back into shape as it cooks. Wrap the chicken loosely in waxed paper and re-frigerate for 3 to 5 hours or overnight.

Preheat oven to 325° F.

Place the chicken in a roasting pan and gently rub some

of the butter over the entire surface. Bake for 1¼ hours, basting and rubbing with the butter every 20 minutes. Sprinkle it with salt. Add the reserved marinade to the pan and continue cooking for 1 hour or until thoroughly done, basting frequently with the pan juices.

Let the chicken stand for 15 to 20 minutes before carving.

Reduce the pan juices over a moderate heat on top of the stove to ½ of the original volume. Spoon a little of the sauce over each portion just before serving.

Makes 4 servings.

Menu

Melons

Consommé de Tomate

Oeufs Froids Colinettes*

Ris de Veau Glacé*

Champignons

Poulets de Grain Rôtis

Baba au Rhum

Chantilly

OEUFS FROIDS COLINETTES
(Cold Poached Eggs in Aspic)

8 eggs
2 truffles, thinly sliced
1 pimiento, thinly sliced
Aspic (see pages 237–238)

* Recipe follows.

Mayonnaise
Watercress sprigs

237

*Newport
Cottages
and Their
"Haute
Cuisine"*

Poach the eggs, basting them as they cook, until the whites are firm and the yolks are thick and covered with a thin film of white. Drain.

Place each egg in a small, flat, oval or round ramekin just a little larger than the egg. Decorate each egg with the truffle and pimiento slices. Cover with a thin layer of the cold, slightly thickened but still liquid Aspic. Refrigerate until the decorations have set.

Fill the ramekins to the brim with the liquid Aspic. Again refrigerate until firm. Garnish with mayonnaise and watercress sprigs.

Makes 8 servings.

Aspic

3¾ cups clear fat-free chicken stock
¼ cup dry white wine
4 envelopes unflavored gelatin
1 teaspoon sugar
2 egg shells, crushed
2 egg whites, lightly beaten
2 tablespoons cognac
Salt

Combine the stock, wine, gelatin, sugar, egg shells, and egg whites. Heat slowly until the mixture comes to a full boil. Remove from the heat and stir in the cognac. Season lightly with salt.

Strain the mixture through a sieve lined with a piece of flannel that has been dipped in cold water and wrung out.

Let stand at room temperature until slightly thickened but still liquid. If the mixture gels before it is used, it may be reheated over a low heat, then cooled again to a slightly thick stage.

Makes 8 servings.

ౘ

RIS DE VEAU GLACÉ
(Individual Ramekins of Sweetbreads in a Rich Sauce with Truffles)

3 pairs sweetbreads
1 quart water
1 teaspoon salt
2 tablespoons lemon juice
4 shallots, peeled and chopped
2 tablespoons butter
2 tablespoons flour
1½ cups milk
½ cup dry white wine
½ teaspoon salt
¼ teaspoon black pepper
1 truffle, thinly sliced
1 egg yolk, lightly beaten
1 tablespoon cognac
2 cups cooked white rice
2 tablespoons melted butter
Paprika

Soak the sweetbreads in ice water to cover for 2 to 3 hours; drain. Place in a saucepan with the 1 quart water, the 1 teaspoon salt, and the lemon juice. Bring to a full boil, then lower the heat and let simmer for 4 minutes. Drain and cover with cold water until cool. Drain again.

Remove all the connective tissues, membranes, and tubes. Cut into thin slices.

Sauté the shallots in the 2 tablespoons butter until limp. Stir in the flour. When the flour is blended, slowly add the milk, stirring as it is added. When the mixture is smooth, add the wine and season with the ½ teaspoon salt and the pepper. Continue to cook, stirring, until the sauce begins to thicken. Add the truffle slices and the sweetbreads. Cook, stirring gently, for 2 to 3 minutes. Add 1 to 2 tablespoons of the hot sauce to the beaten egg yolk in a small bowl. Blend quickly and stir into the hot sauce. Stir in the cognac.

Cover the bottoms of 8 individual ramekins or small shallow baking dishes with the rice. Spoon the sweetbreads and the sauce into each. Top each with a little of the 2 tablespoons melted butter. Place in a heated broiler for a few moments until the surfaces are lightly glazed. Sprinkle with paprika.

Serve at once in the ramekins.

Makes 8 servings.

Menu

Melons

Consommé Carmen*

Chicken Halibut à la Cardinal

Mousseline de Volaille Champignons*

Dindonneaux Rôtis

Gelée de Cranberries

Corn Pudding   Lima Beans

Corbeille aux Mirabelles de Foie Gras

Salade

Bombe Vanille aux Pêches   Sauce Framboise

Gâteaux

* Recipe follows.

ॐ

CONSOMMÉ CARMEN

6 cups clear chicken stock (or broth)
¼ cup long-grained rice, uncooked
1 tablespoon butter
¼ cup chopped onion
½ cup chopped green pepper
1 large tomato, chopped
1 teaspoon tomato puree
¼ cup dry white wine
½ teaspoon dried chervil
Salt

Place the chicken stock in a saucepan and bring to a boil. Add the rice, lower the heat, and allow to simmer until the rice is tender.

Meanwhile, melt the butter and sauté the onion and green pepper in it until limp. Add the tomato, tomato puree, wine, and chervil. Blend, then cook very gently for 30 minutes.

Add to the chicken stock and rice and simmer for 30 minutes. Correct seasoning with salt.

Serve very hot in small bouillon cups.

Makes 6 to 8 small servings.

MOUSSELINE DE VOLAILLE CHAMPIGNONS
(Chicken Mousse with Mushroom Sauce)

6 large fresh mushrooms
1 tablespoon butter
1 tablespoon minced onion
¼ cup dry white vermouth
4 egg yolks
1 cup heavy cream
1 cup ground raw chicken, half dark and half white meat
½ teaspoon salt
¼ teaspoon white pepper
Mushroom Sauce (see page 242)

Preheat oven to 375° F.

Separate the mushroom caps from the stems. Reserve the stems for the Mushroom Sauce. Trim and finely chop the caps.

Melt the butter in a saucepan. Sauté the chopped mushroom caps and onion in it until very soft. Add the vermouth and let simmer until almost all the liquid has evaporated.

Beat the egg yolks with the cream until blended. Add the mushroom and onion mixture and the chicken. Blend and season with the salt and pepper.

Pour the mixture into 8 egg-custard cups. Set the cups in a pan of hot water that comes within 1 inch of the rims of the cups. Place in the preheated oven and bake until firm—about 45 minutes.

Turn out onto small serving plates and spoon the Mushroom Sauce over each serving.

Makes 8 servings.

Mushroom Sauce

2 tablespoons butter
½ cup chopped mushroom stems
1 tablespoon flour
1 cup light cream
¼ cup dry vermouth
¼ cup chicken stock
Salt
Pepper

Melt the butter in a saucepan over a low heat. Add the mushroom stems and cook, stirring, until soft.

Stir in the flour and cook until blended. Slowly add the cream, stirring as it is added. Add the vermouth and stock and continue to stir until the sauce thickens. Season to taste with salt and pepper.

Makes about 1½ cups.

Index